Aksai Chin: An Integral Part of India

Aksai Chin an Integral Part of INDIA

DR. RAMESH PRASAD VERMA

4760-61, 23 ANSARI ROAD
DARYA GANJ
NEW DELHI-110002

AKASHGANGA PRAKASHAN

Aksai Chin: An Integral Part of India

First Edition : 2020

ISBN : 978-93-80527-49-9

Price : ₹ 850/-

Published by

AKASHGANGA PRAKASHAN

4760-61, 23 Ansari Road

Darya Ganj, New Delhi-110002

PRINTED IN INDIA

Preface

Aksai Chin is a disputed border area between China and India since 1950s. India claims that China has occupied approximately 38,000 sq. kms. area of Jammu Kashmir by constructing a road connecting Tibet and Xinjiang around 1957. This development lead to Indo-China war of 1962. India claims that invaded area is part of the Ladakh region of the state of Jammu and Kashmir.

Aksai Chin is mainly a part of Hotan County in Xinjiang Autonomous Region in China. Aksai Chin is a southwestward extension of the Plateau of Tibet. India claims Aksai Chin as a part of the Ladakh region of the state of Jammu and Kashmir.

Because of its remoteness and isolation, Aksai Chin was long an ignored corner of the subcontinent, but the Chinese built a military road through it in the 1950s in order to connect Tibet with Xinjiang. The Indian discovery of the road and objection to the Chinese presence in the sector was one of the factors leading to sharp border clashes between the two countries in 1962. At the conclusion of the conflict, China retained control of about 14,700 square miles (38,000 square km) of territory in Aksai Chin. The area remained a point of contention between the two countries.

Upon independence in 1947, the government of India used the Johnson Line as the basis for its official boundary in the west, which included the Aksai Chin. On 1 July 1954, India's first Prime Minister Jawaharlal Nehru definitively stated the Indian position, claiming that Aksai Chin had been part of the Indian Ladakh region for centuries, and that the border (as defined by the Johnson Line) was non-negotiable. According to George N. Patterson, when the Indian government finally produced a report detailing the alleged proof of India's claims to the disputed area, "the quality of the Indian evidence was very poor, including some very dubious sources indeed". The traditional and customary basis for the border was also presented by the Indian side in the meetings between officials of the governments in 1960. In 1956–57, China constructed a road through Aksai Chin, connecting Xinjiang and Tibet, which ran south of the Johnson Line in many places. Aksai Chin was easily accessible to the Chinese, but access from India, which meant negotiating the Karakoram mountains, was much more difficult. The road came on Chinese maps published in 1958.

This is a reference book. All the matter is just compiled and edited in nature, taken from the various sources which are in public domain.

This book debunks many notions about the boundary dispute and conflict, delves deep into its different aspects to give a blow by blow account of as to how and why a conflict arose over the boundary.

—Editor

Contents

1

Introduction

The western portion of the Sino-Indian boundary originated in 1834, with the Sikh Confederacy's conquest of Ladakh. In 1842, the Sikh Confederacy, which at the time ruled over much of Northern India (including the frontier regions of Jammu and Kashmir), signed a treaty which guaranteed the integrity of its existing borders with its neighbours.

The British defeat of the Sikhs in 1846 resulted in transfer of sovereignty over Ladakh, part of the Jammu and Kashmir region, to the British, and British commissioners contacted Chinese officials to negotiate the border. The boundaries at its two extremities, Pangong Lake and Karakoram Pass, were well defined, but the Aksai Chin area in between lay undefined. W. H. Johnson, a civil servant with the Survey of India, proposed the "Johnson Line" in 1865, which put Aksai Chin in Kashmir.

Johnson presented this line to the Maharaja of Kashmir, who then claimed the 18,000 square kilometres contained within. Johnson's work was severely criticized as inaccurate. His boundary line was described as "patently absurd", and extending further north than the Indian claim.

Johnson was reprimanded by the British Government for crossing into Khotan without permission and resigned from the Survey. According to Francis Younghusband, who explored the region in the late 1880s, there was only an abandoned fort and not one inhabited house at Shahidulla when he was there - it was just a convenient staging post for the nomadic Kirghiz.

The abandoned fort had apparently been built a few years earlier by the Kashmiris. In 1878 the Chinese had reconquered Xinjiang, and by 1890 they already had Shahidulla before the issue was decided. By 1892, China had erected boundary markers at Karakoram Pass.

In 1893, Hung Ta-chen, a senior Chinese official at Kashgar, handed a map of the boundary proposed by China to George Macartney, the British consul-general at Kashgar. This boundary placed the Lingzi Tang plains, which are south of the Laktsang range, in India, and Aksai Chin proper, which is north of the Laktsang range, in China. Macartney agreed with the proposal and forwarded it to the British Indian government.

The British presented this line, known as the Macartney-MacDonald line, to the Chinese in 1899 in a note by SirClaude MacDonald. In 1911 the Xinhai Revolution resulted in power shifts in China, and by the end of World War I, the British officially used the Johnson Line. However they took no steps to establish outposts or assert actual control on the ground. According to Neville Maxwell, the British had used as many as 11 different boundary lines in the region, as their claims shifted with the political situation. From 1917 to 1933, the "Postal Atlas of China", published by the Government of China in Peking had shown the boundary in Aksai Chin as per the Johnson line, which runs along the Kunlun mountains.

Upon independence in 1947, the government of India used the Johnson Line as the basis for its official boundary in the west, which included the Aksai Chin. On 1 July 1954, India's first Prime Minister Jawaharlal Nehru definitively stated the Indian position, claiming that Aksai Chin had been part of the Indian Ladakh region for centuries, and that the border (as defined by the Johnson Line) was non-negotiable. According to George N. Patterson, when the Indian government finally produced a report detailing the alleged proof of India's claims to the disputed area, "the quality of the Indian evidence was very poor, including some very dubious sources indeed". The traditional and customary basis for the border was also presented by the Indian side in the meetings between officials of the governments in 1960. In 1956–57, China constructed a road through Aksai Chin, connecting Xinjiang and Tibet, which ran south of the Johnson Line in many places. Aksai Chin was easily accessible to the Chinese, but access from India, which meant negotiating the Karakoram mountains, was much more difficult. The road came on Chinese maps published in 1958.

THE STRATEGIC SIGNIFICANCE OF ARUNACHAL PRADESH FOR INDIA

The past and contemporary rigidity of China on claiming the whole of the Indian State of Arunachal Pradesh as Chinese territory arises significantly from the strategic importance of this region in relation to China and its hold on Tibet. On the eve of Chinese President Hu Jin Tao's visit to India in 2006 the then Chinese Ambassador to India in a manner that was diplomatically abrasive, unwise and arrogant startled the Indian policy establishment by public assertions that the whole of Arunachal Pradesh was part of China.

"The Strategic Importance of Tawang" Some of the major reasons of the strategic importance of Arunachal Pradesh were highlighted and it was stressed that India could not afford any territorial compromises in this region. In the current season while China has once again focused on rigidly and persistently claiming the whole of this region, it is appropriate to refocus on the strategic importance of Arunachal Pradesh to India. The above referred Paper is reproduced below. Additionally, one would like to stress is that Arunachal Pradesh in India's hands strategically worries China most because it is from this region that India's missile ranges and coverage of Chinese heartland targets, offers the best locations.

Notwithstanding any peace rhetoric from China or efforts to lower temperatures in the India-China border standoff on the Tibet border, it would be realistic for Indian military contingency planning to expect a major Chinese military offensive against India centring on Arunachal Pradesh with Tawang as the initial prime target. That was the lesson of 1962 also.

China: The Strategic Reluctance On Boundary Settlement with India

China ever since its emergence as a monolithic Communist state in 1949 was involved in boundary disputes with virtually every nation on its peripheries. It led to border wars with the former Soviet Union, Vietnam and India. In the case of Vietnam and India, the border wars were perceived by China as punitive wars. China today has undertaken boundary settlements with virtually all countries with which it had disputes with the exception of India. Some in India hoped that with a generational change in leadership in China and with the economic, political and strategic rise of India, China may be prompted to move towards more accommodative stances on the China-India boundary dispute. China's President Hu Jintao would be visiting India from November 20, 2006 for four days. It has been already spelt out, that in terms of perspectives, China has given no indications that India could expect any significant breakthrough announcements by the Chinese president on the boundary dispute. The Chinese President's visit to India in November 2006 will be just one more item in the chronology of China-India relations. A politically correct visit at best.

Endless Round of Border Dispute Negotiations by China

Endless rounds of border dispute negotiations have taken place between China and India. These have taken place at two levels, namely:

Joint Working Group (JWG) discussions which commenced in 1988

Special Representatives talks at the level of India's National Security Advisers and Chinese Vice Minister level since June 2003. The JWG has already completed over fifteen rounds of discussions. The Special Representatives held Seventh Round of talks in March 2006. The standard responses after each round have been of the type that was stated in March 2006: "The two Special Representative continued their discussions for an agreed framework for the resolution of the boundary question in a constructive and friendly atmosphere".

Chinese leaders on visits to India come out with the oft-repeated statement that the boundary dispute should be left to future generations to resolve and meanwhile China-India relations in other fields should move forward. This is just an excuse to keep alive the border dispute as a strategic pressure point against India.

This leads to the question whether China is really serious about resolution of the China-India border dispute? The endless round of negotiations does not suggest so.

It is best exemplified by an Indian media news report that no meetings have been scheduled between Indian and Chinese Special Representatives for talks on the boundary dispute before the visit of Chinese President Hu Jintao on November 20 "as India doesn't expect any substantive progress on the border issue in the near future." Symbolically, China's reluctance can be read as dissatisfaction with growing US-India strategic relationship and keeping alive the border dispute as a strategic pressure point against India. Obviously China is actively involved in delays and prolonging the resolution of the boundary disputes for strategic reasons.

Strategic Reluctance on Boundary Settlement with India by China

Veiled references in the past were made by Indian official spokesmen that progress could not be made as China was constantly pressurizing India to accept a swap by India of Tawang in lieu of Aksai-Chin.

China has now come out in the open to demand and advocate this proposal. An Indian news-report covering the closed door meeting organized between Chinese distinguished experts and Indian academics by China's Institute of Asia-Pacific Studies, which is part of the giant official Chinese Academy of Social Sciences had this to report:

Chinese experts said that China would be magnanimous on the issue of Aksai Chin area if India agreed to give up

Tawang. The high-level Chinese experts which included former Chinese Ambassador to India Chen Rui Sheng made it clear that the border dispute could be solved if India handed over Tawang to China.

The Strategic Significance of Tawang for India

At the outset it must be made clear that for the Chinese, Tawang is not just the Tawang Monastery region. For them Tawang implies the whole of India's Arunachal Pradesh. So as not to dilute their claim, they officially will not call it that Arunachal Pradesh should be returned to them. Coming to the strategic importance of Arunachal Pradesh or Tawang in Chinese parlance the following need to be recognized:

Arunachal Pradesh provides strategic depth to India's Brahmaputra Valley and India's other North Eastern states. Arunachal Pradesh provides security to Bhutan on it entire Eastern flank by geographical contiguity.

Bhutan would be then be in a pincer group of China on both it flanks if Tawang is given away. This would be detrimental to India's security. China's borders would then rest on the plains of Assam; India might as well write off its other North Eastern states. The Chinese obsession with the Tawang Region is totally strategic in its aims.

In any future conflict with China and if India singly or in coalition with some other power develops offensive capabilities against China, this region offers the shortest cut to China proper and to Tibet. India's communications infrastructure in this region developed in World War II for US military aid to China is existent and can be further improved.

Arunachal Pradesh offers all-wealthier lines of communication to India for military needs to the Tibet border as compared to Aksai-Chin. In terms of any air operations by China in this region, Arunachal Pradesh would provide multilayered air defence deployments on the ground as deterrence.

The region is rich in terms of mineral and natural resources prospects. There are many more reasons that one can state but the major ones should be enough. Arunachal Pradesh is of vital strategic importance for the territorial integrity and defence of India's North East states and should be non-negotiable.

China would be politically naive of it perceives that in the 21st Century, a powerfully rising India would accept the bait of a Chinese strategic barter of Aksai-Chin in lieu of Tawang India would be more politically naive than China if it thinks that China would concede the area of Aksai-Chin through which passes its lifelines to keep Xinjiang under Chinese control. Both in Aksai Chin and in the Arunachal Pradesh area, the strategic interests of China and India clash in the most intense manner. It would be a magical wonder if China can turn around to be strategically accommodative of India's strategic sensitivities. China's strategic reluctances to solve the border dispute with India can therefore be expected to bedevil China-India relations for a long time to come.

DOKLAM CHINESE TERRITORY, INDIA SHOULD HAVE LEARNT LESSONS: CHINA

China on Monday said Doklam is a "Chinese territory" and the question of changing the status quo does not arise after India's envoy Gautam Bambawale warned Beijing against any attempt to change the present state of affairs on the plateau.

In an interview to Hong Kong-based *South China Morning Post*, Bambawale said any attempt to change the status quo in Doklam would lead to another stand-off.

The ambassador, however, said both the nations were well within their rights for an army build-up behind the point of the face-off – and the status quo in Doklam remained in place.

Regarding the border issue, China is committed to maintaining peace, stability and tranquillity there and Donglang (Doklam) belongs to China as we have historical conventions. So China's activity there is within its sovereign rights. There is no such thing as changing the status quo.

"Last year, thanks to our concerted efforts, our diplomatic efforts and wisdom that we properly resolved this issue," Hua added. "We hope the Indian side could learn some lessons from this, stick to historical conventions and work with China to ensure the peace and stability in the border area as well as a good atmosphere for the development of bilateral ties," Hua said.

"China and India are exploring ways to resolve their territorial dispute through negotiations so that we can arrive at a mutually acceptable solution and pending the final solution, the two sides should work together and maintain peace and tranquillity in the area."

India and China were locked in a 73-day stand-off at Doklam in the eastern section of their border. The crisis erupted after Indian troops halted road construction at Doka La in the region, citing Bhutan's claim to the area.

Doka La is very close to India's artery which connects its Northeast with the rest of the country. The stand-off was resolved in August.

The ambassador also stressed the need to demarcate the 3,448-km-long disputed border, which is the root cause of friction between India and China.

Talking about the delimitation of the boundary, Hua said:

"China's position is clear and consistent. The east, middle and western side is yet to be officially demarcated. China is committed to resolving the relevant dispute through negotiations."

The long-winding India-China border has three sectors: The western sector between Ladakh and the Chinese-held Aksai Chin; the central sector ranges from Uttarakhand and Tibet; the eastern sector divides Sikkim and Arunachal Pradesh from Tibet.

Asked how China viewed Bambawale's remarks that India does not see China's growing engagement with the South Asian countries as a threat, Hua said: "I commend these positive remarks made by the Indian ambassador. As the two countries are growing at a fast pace, China and India present each other opportunities and also to the world. We share similar national conditions, development goals as well as common interests". "We have every reason to be each other's partners. So we would like to work with India to enhance political trust and mutually beneficial cooperation under the guidance of two leaders (Indian Prime Minister Narendra Modi and Chinese President Xi Jinping) to achieve the common development," said Hua.

CHINA AND INDIA STAND READY TO FIRE AT EACH OTHER: WHAT'S NEXT

Hundreds of troops from China and India, Asia's two largest countries and hardly best friends, are locked in a standoff on the Doklam plateau, a region of the Himalayan mountain kingdom Bhutan where China was apparently building a highway. China fancies that plateau its own. As a protector of Bhutan, India has mobilized up to 10,000 troops "for any contingency," writes Brahma Chellany, professor of Strategic Studies at the New Delhi-based Center for Policy Research, in an opinion piece here. The highway project is off for now, but China's foreign ministry has demanded Indian forces leave before it can hold any talks. China calls the region administered by Bhutan traditional pastureland for Tibetans and controls Tibet itself as a Chinese territory.

It's easy to imagine the standoff since late June will lead to an actual battle between the two countries, who behave something like regional superpowers. Each side's leader has its reputation to defend at home. China figured its claim to the plateau was well established and saw as a "sign of arrogance" that India would marshal its forces given that it lags the Chinese in economic, military and social indices, says Mohan Malik, professor at the Asia-Pacific Center for Security Studies in Honolulu.

But each side will probably just hold tight to scope out the other from a distance until the governments can talk. "The track record for calming border tensions between China and India is normally quite good," says Sameer Lalwani, deputy director for The Stimson Center think tank's South Asia program. He cites a 1986 standoff that lasted 10 months until solved through high-level talks. Today's standoff could "peter out" as colder weather sets in, proceed to formal talks if Indian troops pull back or "deepen but remain stable with both sides digging in, making permanent their military positions and infrastructure," he says.

China and India are ominously used to these standoffs, reducing the odds of armed conflict. Both have learned to live with grey zones in the Himalayas dividing them, neither conceding nor pushing the other side out. They most obviously dispute two regions, Aksai Chin and part of Arunachal Pradesh, with China controlling the former and India holding the latter.

Still, the Doklam standoff in Bhutan, a country that called neighboring India for support this time, comes amid particularly virulent Chinese protests and as India pushes back more broadly against Chinese control in the region. It's helping Vietnam resist Beijing's hold in the disputed South China Sea even though it lacks a claim there and it's even building a north-south trade corridor that would rival China's "Silk Road" for economic co-development with other countries. There's always a chance of miscalculation or accident on the Doklam plateau, Lalwani notes.

But the two sides that fought a month-long border war in 1962 signed an agreement 31 years later to maintain harmony even as disputes fester. Troop standoffs in 2013 and 2014 were "pretty tense," Chellany tells Forbes. Yet they didn't go to war. This standoff probably won't either. Officials in New Delhi say it can be resolved without "muscle flexing," according to Indian media reports.

You hear a lot of vocal chord flexing, of course. China's Huanqiu.com news website reported in Chinese Sunday that India must withdraw "illegal" border troops and asked whether it was "really prepared" to fight a war with China at 10,000 feet above sea level. An Indian legislator was quoted on the Indian News Express Wednesday website saying China has planted a nuclear bomb in Pakistan with the intent to strike India.

But dialogue at least at the quiet, informal level is expected before those words translate to actions. Indian National Security Advisor Ajit Doval is already scheduled to visit Beijing by month's end. Ministers from both are meeting for regional trade talks in India, as well, despite the border bugaboo.

"The only possible solution to the current standoff is for the Chinese and Indian sides to withdraw from Bhutan's Doklam plateau," Chellany says. "It will also allow China to save face while safeguarding Bhutan's territorial interests." Eventually, he says, the two sides should hold "unpublicized negotiations...to defuse the current crisis and work out a mutual retreat."

2

The Puzzle of Aksai Chin

In the western sector of the China-India border, the dispute has centred on the Aksai Chin area. The British left Aksai Chin area as "undefined" at the time of their transfer of power in 1947.nehru himself once stated that " it is a matter of argument as to what art of it (Aksai Chin) belongs to us and what part of it belongs to somebody else.... The point is, there has never been any delimitation there in that area and it has been a challenged area." Before the British left India, the British-Indian government had shown no boundary at all in that area on its official maps.

In Volume XII of Aichison'd Treaties published in 1931, it was stated that"The northern as well as the eastern boundary of the Kashmir state is still undefined." The Survey of India maps published in the 1900s and 1930s did not indicate any boundary alignment or show any colour difference in this are, and wide spaces between Kashmir and Xinjiang and between Kashmir and Tibet were shown blank. Louis Dane, Indian Foreign Secretary, stated clearly in a letter to the Indian office that Aksai Chin was I Chinese Xinjiag. The neighbourhood of the Lanak Pass at the head of the Changchenmo valley was supposed to be the most northerly boundary point on the Kashmir-Tibet border.

In 1945, guided by Olaf Caroe, then foreign secretary of India, on new Survey of India maps the Aksai Chin area began to be shown by a colour-wash with the words "Boundary

Undefined" marked on it. In 1947, the Indian Army in its "top secret" m submitted to the British Cabinet Mission accepted the Karakoram range as the northern boundary of India in the western sector.

However, after the signing of the trade agreement concerning Tibet in 1954, following Nehru's instructions, new Survey of India maps began to show an international boundary in the western sector running along the crest of the Kunlun range, which for the first time placed the whole Aksai Chin area within the Indian territory. According to Sir H.A.F. Rumbold, an official in the Indian Office, the Simon Commission wished to include a map of India in Volume I of their report in 1929. Rumbold found nothing in the India office to justify the line on the Kunlun range shown on some maps. The Commission accordingly adopted a line roughly along the crest of the Karakoram range, excluding the Aksai Chin area. Nehru, even on August 28, 1959, stated in the Lok Sabha that "This was the boundary of the old Kashmir state with Tibet and Chinese Turkestan. Nobody had marked it."

On the other hand, Chinese maps have shown the Karakoram range as its boundary in the western sector at least since the 1920s. There was no evidence that the British-Indian authorities ever disputed this with the Chinese government before they left India in 1947. The widely accepted modern concept of boundary marking involes three steps: delimitation, delineation and demarcation. Delimitation involves defining the boundary in written terms through treaties and agreements. Delineation involves sketching the boundary in maps through joint boundary surveys. Demarcation involves marking the boundary line on the ground through pillars, chains and other markers.

Reviewing the historic facts for the entire China-India border, such a China-India boundary has never existed, though each side has made its own territorial claims. Historical facts have also showed that, in the old days, wide desolate tracts in the remote high mountains between the two countries were physically inaccessible. Therefore, the China-India border dispute has been the dispute on the "zone" rather than the " line" in the eastern and western sectors. Mutual understanding and recognition of such historical evolution of the China-India border should become the starting point for the future border deliberations.

The Sino/Indian Dispute

Ever since its establishment in 1949, the attitude of the Communist Chinese Government towards India has been bound up with the Tibetan issue. India had, on gaining independence in 1947, inherited the British "special position" in Tibet, along with the Mission in Lhasa and trade agencies in larger towns. It had retained the services of British officials stationed in Tibet. When, in 1949, Tibetan leaders made their bid to contact foreign Governments, they first contacted these officials, and it was only a short step for the suspicious minded Chinese to regard this as evidence of Indian collusion with the British.

The Communist Chinese also had ideological reasons for believing that such collusion existed. At the time of their coming to power, Moscow was propagating the line of a world divided into two camps, with the Indian Government depicted as a tool of British imperialism and firmly situated in the opposing camp. The Communist Chinese leaders, who previously had little contact with the outside world, faithfully repeated these accusations against Nehru and his Government. The Chinese occupation of Tibet in late 1950, Peking's suspicions of the Indians were further aroused when Nehru, in notes to the Chinese Government, expressed the "surprise and regret" of his Government at the Chinese action. He described as "deplorable" the Chinese use of force in Tibet.

Standard diplomatic practice stipulates that a state does not criticise the behaviour of another state acting within its own territorial boundaries unless there are special reasons for so doing. The Indians justified their criticism of the Chinese on the ground of their special interest in Tibet, from which the Chinese inferred that the Indians were implying some restriction on Chinese sovereignty. A sharp reply was received from the

Chinese accusing the Indians of unwarranted interference and claiming that the policy of the Indian Government was "affected by foreign influences hostile to China in Tibet".

Nevertheless, whatever suspicions the Chinese may have felt about the Indians in 1949-50 must to some extent have been allayed by subsequent developments. India opposed the 1950 Tibetan appeal to the United Nations; it was one of the few non-communist countries not to condemn China's intervention in the Korean War; it sought to have China seated an the United Nations. The culmination of these moves to improve relations with China was the signing, in April 1954, of an agreement by which India recognised without qualification China's sovereignty over Tibet and conceded many of India's former rights there. A few months later the Chinese Premier, Chou En-lai, paid a successful visit to India, and in October of the same year Nehru visited Peking.

The very considerable improvement in Sino/Indian relations from 1950 to 1954 was on the Indian side almost entirely the result of efforts by Nehru, who saw friendship between China and India as the starting point of a new order in world affairs. It must have been obvious to the Chinese that considerable opposition to Nehru's pro-China policies, at least as far as Tibet was concerned, existed both within and outside the Indian Government. It should also have been clear that problems were going to arise over wide discrepancies in the claimed Sino/ Indian border, as shown in maps published by both sides.

However, as long as Nehru's China policy appeared to produce results, his opposition in India remained silent. It was important for both Nehru and the Chinese that this policy continued to appear to give results, and hence the efforts made by both sides to keep intact the edifice of good relations. The Chinese, under the 1954 agreement, allowed India to maintain certain trade and pilgrimage rights in Tibet. They sought to play down the significance of border differences, stating that they had simply inherited their claimed Sino/Indian frontier from the pre-1949 Nationalist Government and that it would be "revised" in due course. Nehru, for his part, avoided public mention of the reality and extent of border differences, and it seemed that both sides were moving towards a compromise settlement of the question.

What were these differences, and what evidence was there that both sides were in fact prepared to compromise? The Sino/Indian border can be divided into three sectors: (i) an eastern sector where 99,000 square kilometres of territory described by the Indians as the Northeast Frontier Agency, or N.E.F.A is in dispute: (ii) a middle sector where some 2.000 square kilometres of territory on either side of the main Himalayan passes is disputed: and (iii) a western sector where the Indian province of Ladakh borders on Tibet and Sinkiang and where both the Indian/Tibet and Indian/Sinkiang borders are disputed, in particular the ownership of some 30,000 square kilometres of high plateau country known as the Aksai Chin.

To an outside observer looking at the frontier as it stands, an apparent basis for a compromise settlement would be for China to drop its claim to the N.E.F.A. in exchange for India dropping its claim to the Aksai Chin, with both sides making concessions over the middle sector and the Ladakh/Tibetan border. Such a settlement accords with the realities of both geography and administrative control two important criteria in the settlement of border disputes. The N.E.F.A. lies to the south of the Himalayan watershed and is controlled by India. The Aksai Chin, for the most part, lies to the north of the main range, and the Chinese claim to have controlled the area since 1950. In 1956-7, they built a strategic road across the Aksai Chin, linking Sinkiang with Tibet. That the Indians learnt about the road only from a map published by the Chinese in 1958 is substantial evidence that India was not in control of the area. The historical basis of the border is more confused. The Indian claim to the N.E.F.A. rests almost entirely on acceptance of the McMahon Line, a line agreed to by the Tibetans and British in 1914 as the border in this area.

In the Aksai Chin area no agreement has ever been reached on the alignment of the border. Nevertheless, if both sides were to take a generous view of the historical data, a basis for a

N.E.F.A./Aksai Chin exchange could be found. During the post-1954 honeymoon period of Sino/Indian relations, both sides did in fact seem prepared to take a generous view of the situation and to move towards a compromise settlement. In 1956, Chou En-lai admitted privately to Nehru that, although lie thought the McMahon line "was not fair", nevertheless China would accept the line as the border with India after they had "consulted with the Tibetan authorities". Chinese recognition of the McMahon Line was also implied when its eastern extension was accepted as a basis for border negotiations with Burma, and by Chinese de facto acceptance of the line as the dividing line between Chinese and Indian forces in the area.

Nehru, for his part, appeared willing to play down the Indian claims to the Aksai Chin. He tried to delay disclosure if the news that the Chinese had built a road in the area. After the news had been revealed, he sought to play down the economic significance of the area, describing it as a "barren tundra". He even went so far as to cast doubt on the validity of the Indian claim to the area. In statements to the Indian Parliament during early 1959, Nehru pointed out that "during British rule, this area was neither inhabited: nor were there any outposts", adding that "this place, Aksai Chin area, is distinguish completely from other areas. It is a matter for argument which part belongs to us and which part belongs to somebody else. It is not clear".

Nehru's efforts to take the heat out of the Aksai Chin question were not entirely successful. (One of his critics even suggested building an atomic reactor in the area to promote its economic development.) News of the Chinese road in the area appeared to trigger off long-suppressed Indian sensitivity over the border issue, and, in August 1958, the Indian Government made a formal claim to the disputed territory in all three sectors.

In a letter to Nehru of January 1959, Chou En-lai claimed that the Aksai Chin was Chinese territory and added that the McMahon Line was a "product of British aggression", illegal, and had "never been recognised by the Chinese Central

Government". He proposed that the existing status quo he maintained, however, pending a negotiated settlement of the dispute, and added that China would take a "realistic attitude" over the McMahon Line.*

The Tibetan uprising of March 1959 upset the delicate balance of Sino/Indian relations. Reports of Chinese military action to suppress the uprising, together with the sight of thousands of Tibetan refugees crossing into Indian territory, quickly aroused feelings of alarm and anger in India, particularly among those who believed their country had an historic interest in Tibet.

Nehru's Right-Wing critics charged that India should never have allowed the Chinese into Tibet in the first place. Nehru, influenced possibly both by Indian public opinion and his own feelings on the question, came out in open condemnation of Chinese behaviour in Tibet.

The Chinese reacted even more strongly than they had in 1950. Nehru, in addition to condemning the Chinese, had spoken of his sympathy with "the aspirations of the Tibetans for autonomy". He had given asylum to the Dalai Lama, who was also allowed facilities to make his 1959 appeal for U. N. action over Tibet. And finally, the Chinese had reason to believe that the Tibetan guerrillas were receiving arms from across the Indian border.

In May 1959 the Chinese published a long article urging, almost begging, Nehru not to be swayed by his reactionary Right-Wing critics and to return to the path of Sino/Indian friendship.

With a frankness and detail probably unmatched by any other Chinese statement on foreign policy, the article set out the Chinese case over Tibet, and accused the Indians of unjustified interference. Indian trade with Tibet was greatly restricted. Clashes involving casualties occurred at several points along the disputed border as the Chinese Army extended its control over border areas in an effort to restrict the movecourt of Tibetans across the frontier.

These border clashes, following in the wake of the Tibetan uprising, appeared to put an end to Nehru's willingness to compromise over the border dispute. Having earlier in 1959 cast doubt on the Indian claim to the Aksai Chin, in September he stated before the Indian Parliament that the Chinese claims were "absurd" and would mean "handing over the Himalayas to them as a gift". A Chinese call in November 1959 for negotiations and a twenty-kilometre military withdrawal from the McMahon Line in the east and the "line of actual control" in the west to prevent a recurrence of border clashes was met with an Indian demand for a prior Chinese withdrawal from the Aksai Chin. A Chinese reply pointing out that this should also be paralleled by an Indian withdrawal from the NE.F.A. was ignored. In the end the Chinese appeared to settle for a freezing of the existing status quo - without negotiations or a twenty-kilometre withdrawal.

However, if the Chinese were happy to keep things as they were (keeping also their road across the Aksai Chin), Nehru and his Government were not. Throughout 1960-61 Indian opinion progressively hardened, and demands for the Government to do something about Tibet and the disputed border increased. The army was given full control over the frontier districts and it proceeded to build up its strength in these areas. During the summer (northern) of 1962, Indian military patrols repeatedly crossed the Chinese-claimed line of actual control in the western sector of the frontier. Posts were established well behind the Chinese forward positions in territory claimed and occupied by the Chinese. Frequent and insistent Chinese protests were met with the bald statement that the Indians were merely operating in Indian territory. By August 14, Nehru was able to announce that India had three times as many posts in the western sector as the Chinese. He asked for a free hand to continue the build-up of Indian strength in the area.

The Chinese had repeatedly warned that a continuation of such activity would end in hostilities. On July 9, they had warned the Indians "to rein in on the brink of the precipice".

On August 4, they called for immediate negotiations on the border. The Indians replied that negotiations could not be held until the Chinese had ceased their occupation of "every square inch of sacred Indian territory", and that the Chinese must first "vacate their aggression" in the Aksai Chin. The Chinese replied on September 13 proposing talks to begin on October 15 "without preconditions", that is, without a Chinese withdrawal from the Aksai Chin. The Indians refused the offer.

While Indian military pressure was building up along the Chinese-claimed border in the western sector, a curious situation was developing along the McMahon Line in the eastern sector. The Indians claim that at its western end the McMahon Line was not accurately drawn: that it was meant to have followed the crest of a line of hills known as the Thag La ridge. The Chinese claim, and have produced the original McMahon Line from the Tibetan archives to prove their point, that the line as originally drawn lies approximately twelve miles south of this ridge along the southern side of a small river valley. (Western maps show the McMahon Line in conformity with the Chinese claim.) The area between the Indian and Chinese versions of the McMahon Line is described by the Indians as the Dho La strip. This was not the only unilateral revision of the McMahon Line carried out by the Indians. In his letter to Chou En-lai of September 29, 1959, Nehru admitted that in the Migyitun area (to the east of the Dho La strip) the border shown on Indian maps "differs slightly from the boundary shown in the Treaty map". He claimed that when the McMahon line was drawn, "the exact topographical features in this area were not known". The Indians have also now come to admit that "blind adherence" to the original McMahon Line would leave the Dho La strip on the Chinese side at the border.

It is not clear who first occupied the Dho La strip. The Chinese claim that the area had always been under their control and that Indian troops moved in during 1962. The Indians claim they had long occupied the area and that the Chinese began a to establish posts in the area after September 8, 1962. What is clear is that on October 12, 1962, Nehru announced in the Indian Parliament that he had given the order to drive the Chinese out of the Dho La strip.

Eight days later, on October 20, the Chinese attacked in force across the Thagla La ridge and into the disputed strip, while advancing their troops into the Chinese-claimed territory in the western sector where the Indians had earlier established posts. Four days later, the Chinese called for a ceasefire to be followed by a withdrawal of both sides from the line that separated them at that moment (the so-called October 24 line of actual control).

Failing to get a satisfactory response from the Indians, they advanced troops south of the Dho La strip into the N.E.F.A., defeating Indian military forces in the area. Two weeks later, they withdrew to the positions occupied on October 24. The main point of contention between the Chinese and Indians ever since has been whether the Chinese should maintain their October 24 positions or withdraw further to the positions they occupied before fighting broke out.

The Chinese attack of October 1962 has led to an almost complete breakdown in relations between China and India. The level of each country's diplomatic representation in the other has been greatly reduced. Many thousands of Chinese nationals have been expelled from India. The few Indian nationals living in China have, in one way or another, been forced to leave. Border incidents have continued. Both sides have launched extreme propaganda campaigns against each other, the Chinese denouncing Nehru as a representative of the "big bourgeoisie" and a tool for U. S. aggressive designs against Tibet, while the Indians denounce the Chinese for having aggressive, imperialist designs against Indian territory. Both sides have gone to great lengths to discredit each other inter- nationally. Both sides have increased their military preparedness along the Himalayan frontier, particularly India, which has doubled its military budget to a level it cannot afford.

The question thus arises: Who is primarily to blame for the hostility in Sino/Indian relations? From the account already given, the primary cause of the hostility was the post-1959 dispute over the Sino/Indian border leading to the Chinese attack of October 20. But why the sudden emergence of such a dispute between two countries previously enjoying good relations? Reverting to the terminology of our previous discussion on hostility between states, both sides see the breakdown in relations as being caused by the active hostility of the other side. This hostility, they claim, is both ideologically and national- interest based. The Chinese are accused of having acted in a hostile manner out of a desire to acquire territory and out of strong ideological dislike for the Indian Government. The Chinese claim the Indians have designs against Chinese territory and that their Government is under the influence of anti-Chinese and pro-U. S. reactionary elements.

Both sides realise that they have somehow or other to explain why the other side suddenly, in 1959, decided that its interests were no longer served by the maintenance of normal relations. The Indian explanation is that Chinese pre-1959 policy was designed to lull India into a false sense of security and so facilitate Chinese ambitions. The Chinese explanation was that reactionary elements began to gain the upper hand in the Indian Government in 1959, and point to the post-1959 increase in U. S. aid to India as evidence.

In fact there is good reason to believe that the hostility shown by each side towards the other was reactive rather than active: that each side was reacting to the believed hostility of the other. To take the Chinese side of things first.

In terms of the account already given, it seems likely that the Chinese attack of October 20, 1962, was primarily a reaction to Indian military pressure along the disputed frontier during preceding months. It could be argued, however. that the behaviour of the Chinese before October 20, and in particular their propaganda attacks against the Indians from 1960 onwards, cannot be explained simply as a reaction to previous events: that overall Chinese behaviour must therefore include some aggressive component.

The Chinese had in fact made their first hostile move against the Indians back in 1959 when they restricted Indian trading and other rights in Tibet. The Chinese had also, according to the Indians, extended somewhat the area they claimed in the western sector. And they had, according to the Indians, been responsible for the 1959 border clashes already mentioned. The Indian charge is based on alleged differences between the frontier claimed by the Chinese to 1956 and that shown on a map of the claimed Sino/Indian frontier handed to the Indians by the Chinese in 1960. The Chinese deny any difference between the two lines.

Unless these apparently hostile acts of the Chinese can be explained in reactive terms., in terms of their reacting to previous Indian actions, then it would seem that the Chinese had taken the initiative in hostility towards India and were largely responsible for the eventual breakdown in relations.

The hardening of the Chinese attitude towards India in 1959 was clearly related to Tibetan developments in that year. In judging the behaviour of the Chinese, we need, in effect, to ask whether their sensitivity over Tibet was sufficient to explain this hardening of attitude.

To accept that the Communist Chinese are, in fact extremely sensitive toward Tibet does not necessarily imply a simple acceptance of Chinese propaganda. What we know of Chinese thinking and behaviour, strongly suggests that this sensitivity does exist. If all non-communist Chinese believe that China has the right to consider Tibet as an integral part of her territory, we should accept that Communist Chinese are equally convinced. If many non-communist Chinese believe (as they do) that Britain had designs against Tibet, we should accept that Communist Chinese, educated to believe in the evils of US Western imperialism, will be at least equally fearful. We do not need accept that these views are correct; we may even consider they are absurd. But if we are going to get anywhere in trying to understand China's behaviour, we should start from the assumption that these views may be sincerely hold in Peking.

Nor may it be so absurd for the Communist Chinese to think along these lines. The Chinese legal claim to Tibet, it has been argued, appears difficult to refute. As for fears of foreign designs, if the British had earlier convinced themselves that the activities of one Russian agent in Lhasa could lead the politically unstable Tibetans to ally themselves with Tsarist Russia, the Chinese could be excused for thinking that the presence of a British Mission in Lhasa dealing directly with the independent-minded Tibetans and arranging on occasion for the supply of arms from India was evidence of British ambitions eventually to detach Tibet from China, and that India may have inherited these ambitions.

Similarly, it would not be entirely surprising if the Chinese viewed the supply of foreign arms to Tibetan guerrillas from northern India in 1959 as confirmation that such ambitions existed. Finally, the Chinese were hound to be impressed by the demands of the Indian Right Wing for action against the Chinese in Tibet.

For example: some weight could be attached to the fact that the then Chief of the Indian Army Staff wrote a not unenthusiastic foreword for a book published in 1961 entitled The Chinese Aggression. The author of the hook, a Dr. Satyanarayan Sinha, predicted that the "clash of the Indochinese weapons for the possession of the Himalayas will lead to making Tibet an independent country again", and suggested ways in which this could be done.

These, then, are the reasons for believing the Chinese may he sensitive about Tibet. Chinese behaviour provides further confirmation. British officials captured in Tibet in 1950 were subjected to long imprisonment and continual interrogation - treatment far more severe than that meted out to British nationals who fell into communist hands elsewhere in China. And there was Nehru's sad admission to the Indian Parliament in 1959 after talks with Chou En-Iai, of the Chinese having "some sort of kink in their minds... of foreign countries, United Kingdom or America, somehow making incursions into Tibet".

In sum, therefore, it does not seem unreasonable to conclude that the Communist Chinese sincerely believed they had a right to Tibet and that their position in the area was threatened from the direction of India. In which case they would have interpreted Indian behaviour in 1959 as an indication of hostility to which they felt compelled, or entitled, to react.

However, if Chinese behaviour in 1959 can be explained in reactive terms, can the same be said about the Chinese attack of October 1962? Even if the Indian claim to the Dho La strip was doubtful, does not the violence and intensity of the 1962 attack suggest that China was doing more than retaliate for any wrongs she may have believed the Indians to base committed? By 1962, the Chinese were confronted not only by Indian agitation over Tibet, but also by two further aspects of Indian behaviour which would even more easily have been misunderstood. They were: (i) the Indian military build-up along the Sino/Indian border in 1961-2 and (ii) rigid Indian insistence that, as a precondition to border negotiations, the Chinese must first evacuate the whole of the Aksai Chin.

At the time, the Indians justified their position on negotiations and their military build up in terms of the correctness of their border claims. Indeed, the official Indian position was that the line claimed by India as a border had already been defined historically, and that the only purpose of negotiations was to demarcate on the ground the exact alignment of this border.

From this it followed that they were justified (a) in regarding rival Chinese claims, and the occupation of the Aksai Chin, as evidence of Chinese hostility, and (b) in insisting that occupied territory had to be vacated before there could be negotiations. In the meantime the Indians had no alternative but to use military means to counter the Chinese "aggression".

If India was in fact the injured party in the territorial dispute, the Indian attitude over the disputed border would have been explicable at least to an impartial observer, and possibly even to the less impartial Chinese. There would be less justification for the Chinese reacting in the way they did. But was this the case? To answer this question we need to take a closer look at the historical background to the Sino /Indian frontier, and shall begin with the eastern sector, or N.E.F.A.

Until the 1920's, the region now known as the N.E.F.A. was largely unexplored. It was, and still is, inhabited by tribes of Tibeto-Burmese origin, some of which enjoyed trade and tributary relations with Tibet. Certain areas in the north of the region, the Tawang district for example, were inhabited by Tibetans and were under administrative control from Tibet.

The McMahon Line was negotiated with the Tibetans in 1914 at the time of the Simla Conference. It was drawn as far to the north as possible, since the British at the time sought to forestall a feared Chinese expansion into the foothills bordering the Assam plains. The McMahon Line as part of a bargain whereby the British would press the Chinese to concede territory elsewhere to Tibet.

Even so, the Tibetans were not entirely happy about losing territory south of the McMahon Line, the Tawang district in particular. Their acceptance of the line was conditional on possible future adjustments in their favour. No such adjustments, were ever made.

The British also failed to extract the promised concessions from the Chinese, since the latter refused to accept the Convention produced at the Simla Conference. Thus, even as a Tibetan/British frontier, the McMahon Line does not have full validity, particularly as the Tibetans subsequently, in 1936, made a formal request to the British for revision of the line in their favour a request which the British ignored. As late as 1946, the Tibetans were still collecting taxes in the Tawang area. And, in 1947, the Tibetans approached the newly established Indian Government, seeking the "return" of "Tibetan territories" from Assam to Ladakh.

The Indian reply to this approach may be of interest in the light of complaints to be voiced later by the Indians over the manner in which the Chinese spoke of their border claims being inherited from previous Chinese Governments "The Government of India should be glad to have an assurance that it is the intention of the Tibetan Government to continue relations an the existing basis until new Agreements are any reached... This is the procedure adopted by all other countries with which India has inherited Treaty relations from His Majesty's Government".

The validity of the McMahon Line as a Chinese/Indian frontier is considerably more doubtful. True, in rejecting the draft Simla Contention, the Chinese did not specifically object to the McMahon Line as drawn on the map of Tibet attached to the Convention. But, as the Chinese point out, the then Chinese Government had no way of knowing what this line was supposed to represent, since the terms of the McMahon Line agreement were for some reason kept secret by the British and Tibetans until 1929. It could, in theory, have been a border between Tibet and a Chinese-owned N.E.F.A. Moreover, Chiang Kaishek's Government was later to make it clear to the British (and the Indians after 1947) that it did not accept the McMahon Line. The Chinese have also pointed out that, since neither the British nor the Chinese regarded Tibet as a sovereign entity, the Tibetans were obliged to obtain Chinese approval for any frontier negotiated with a foreign power. * Failure to obtain this approval, both at the Simla Conference and later, meant that the McMahon Line never at any stage enjoyed international legality. And finally, as the Chinese never tire of pointing out, many Western and Indian maps, including one reproduced in a book by Nehru himself, Discovery of India, have, even in recent years., shown the Sino/Indian border as running along the edge of the Assam plain in conformity with the traditional Chinese claim.

The 1906 Convention between Britain and China had required China to accept responsibility for Tibet's foreign relations. "The 1907 Anglo/Russian Convention required Britain 'not to enter into negotiations with Tibet except through the intermediary of the Chinese Government". Negotiations with the Tibetans over the McMahon Line were thus a breach of both conventions - a possible reason why the terms of the McMahon Line agreement were kept secret.

For the Communist Chinese to appear to be willing to drop their N.E.F.A. claim is no small concession in view of the very considerable doubts as to the validity of the McMahon Line. Indeed, the Nationalist Government in Taiwan feels so strongly shout the justice of the Chinese clams that its official newspapers have accused Peking of being willing to abandon "sacred" Chinese territory. They have predicted that the present Communist Chinese leaders will be condemned by future generations of Chinese for their betrayal of China's interests. Nevertheless, the Indian position was that the Chinese should not only drop their claim to the N.E.F.A. but to the Aksai Chin also. How strong is the Indian claim in the western sector of the disputed frontier?

The province of Ladakh, which lies on the Indian side of the disputed western sector, was originally a semi-independent state with a complex tributary relationship with Tibet. It was far from being clearly defined Indian territory. These links with Tibet were severed as a result of the 1841 invasion of Tibet from Kashmir, and Ladakh was incorporated into India. In the agreement which followed the invasion, the Ladakh/Tibet border was defined simply as following "the old established frontier", and it was only subsequently that British cartographers decided where this frontier should lie. A small area lying between the Chinese-claimed and Indian-claimed frontiers is in dispute.

By far the larger area in dispute, the Aksai Chin, lies for the most part north of the Ladakh/Tibet frontier, and its ownership depends on a definition of the Ladakh/Sinkiang border. At the end of the nineteenth century, the British decided an effort should be made to define this border, and in 1899 a note was delivered to the Chinese suggesting a possible alignment.

This alignment is shown on the map above, and it will be seen that it leaves with China much of the territory at present in dispute. The Chinese never replied to the note. Shortly afterwards, the British attitude changed.

Alarmed by growing Chinese weakness in Central Asia, and fearing Russian expansion into the area (fears similar to those being entertained in connection with Tibet), the British felt they should establish the border as far north as possible to forestall any southward advance by the Russians. British maps began to show the border as lying far to the north along the Kun Lun mountains. Chinese agreement was never sought for this claimed border (despite the fact that the British recognised Chinese sovereignty in Sinkiang) ; presumably it was only being put forward as an emergency measure in case the Russians attempted to seize Sinkiang. By the 1920's the Russian threat had disappeared, and it was deemed safe to drop this particular claim.

In subsequent years, British and Indian maps showed a variety of claim lines some coinciding with the present Chinese claim line, some the claim line along the Kun Lun mountains, and some an in-between claim line which ran south of the Kun Lun mountains but which included the Aksai Chin as Indian territory.

Maps showing this last claim line were in general use at the time of the 1947 transfer of power, and appear to constitute the basis of the present Indian claim to the Aksai Chin. However, the only border to have ever been officially proposed to the Chinese by the British in this area was that of 1899, and, as already mentioned, this border left most of the Aksai Chin with China.

Whatever the merits of rival Chinese and Indian claims to the Aksai Chin area, it does seem clear that the Indians can hardly speak of the frontier they claim in this area as being already defined by history and therefore subject only to demarcation.

In this connection a rather curious aspect of the Indian position should be mentioned - an aspect which has been overlooked by most students of the Sino/Indian dispute.

Numerous Indian authorities, including Nehru himself, have claimed historical validity for their version of the Indian! Sinkiang frontier on the ground that the line proposed by the British in 1899 "ran along the Kun Lun range to a point east of 80° longitude, where it met the eastern boundary of Ladakh". In fact, the 1899 line ran well to the south of the Kun Lun mountains, and the text of the proposal speaks only of the tine meeting "the spur running south from the Kun Lun range, which [the spur] has hitherto been shown on our maps as the eastern boundary of Ladakh. This is a little east of 80° east longitude".* A misquotation of these dimensions is rather serious, particularly when it is used to justify an official claim to some 30,000 square kilometres of territory, and when, on the basis of this claim, negotiations are refused in favour of a military solution of a complex border dispute.

The only observer who appears to have noted this misquotation is Alastair Lamb. In his book, *The China-India Border*, he gives the full text of the British note of 1899 and lists some of the Indian authorities who have misquoted the 1899 proposal. Distribution of his book within India has been banned.

It would seem, therefore, that an impartial observer who takes into account not only the historical background of the border dispute, but also the equally relevant criteria of geography and administrative control, would agree that the Chinese are not being unreasonable when they call for border negotiations on the basis of the present status quo.

If, as seems to be the case, the Chinese are prepared to do a N.E.F.A./Aksai Chin exchange leaving India in control of far the largest and most valuable of the territories in dispute, he may even feel that the Chinese are being quite generous. And if our impartial observer were to reach such a conclusion, it seems highly likely that the Chinese would be convinced of the reasonableness of their position and the unreasonableness of the Indian demand for a unilateral Chinese withdrawal from the Aksai Chin.

If the Chinese were in fact convinced that they were in the right over the border dispute, they would in all probability have interpreted the Indian military build-up along the disputed border in 1961-2 as evidence of active hostility.

Striking confirmation that this was the case is contained in the "Tibetan Documents" - official Chinese documents which were captured by Tibetan rebels in 1961 and which subsequently found their way to the U.S., where they have been translated and published.

These documents were intended as background briefing to senior Chinese military commanders stationed along the Sino/Indian border. As such, their contents cannot be dismissed simply as propaganda. The documents warned of U.S./Indian collusion to build up pressure along the Tibetan frontier as a prelude to a joint attack against Tibet. Military commanders were instructed to observe strictly the twenty-kilometre troop withdrawal from the line of actual control and to avoid clashes with advancing Indian patrols since this would provide the "imperialists" with the pretext they needed to justify their planned attack.

THE FUTURE OF CHINA'S REGIONAL STRATEGY AND ITS IMPLICATION

What could change the current course? Two external factors, dynamically linked with the debate on "peace and development" inside China, will shape China's regional strategy in the future.

U.S. Perceptions and U.S.-China Interactions

Because the U.S. remains at the centre of China's strategic calculus, the first external factor that is going to influence the future of China's regional strategy is U.S. long-term strategic intentions toward China and how Washington views China's interaction with regional countries. What the United States is doing, plans to do, or even is rumoured to do, will influence China's behavior.

In dealing with the U.S., however, China faces a conundrum that cannot be easily overcome.

Because there will always be voices inside the United States arguing that China will become an inevitable foe, and they continue to view any perceived or real increase of Chinese influence in the region as detrimental to U.S. interest (at least potentially) through the zero-sum prism, China faces a difficult balancing act in dealing with regional states and building a regional order: If China remains an outsider, these people in the U.S. will take it as a sign that China is a challenge to international norms and order (or status quo). If China actively participates in regional affairs and norms, they will again take it as a sign that China is to challenge U.S. dominance—this time, through building a regional sphere of influence. Either way, China is in a no-win situation. At the same time, international politics is becoming more regional, this again puts China in a difficult situation in front of a U.S. audience, in all three possible scenarios. The first scenario is that even though many regional initiatives are not China's idea originally, China has to actively participate in them for fearing of being left out (for instance, the ARF and ASEAN plus Three, or APT). But if China decides to join, its weight in these initiatives will grow, and the U.S. may deem it threatening. Second, there are some regional programs that did come from China's initiatives, but these initiatives are actually designed to assure regional states of China's benign intention (e.g. ASEAN-China FTA, and recent proposal to form an East Asian military dialogue). Nonetheless, because these initiatives came from China, they will arouse U.S. suspicion. Finally, there are initiatives (e.g. SCO) that do have more flavor of limiting U.S. influence. The problem is that the U.S. will pay attention only to the bad part, even though they may evolve into a regional stabilizing force later.

On the other hand, China over the years has come to recognize that regional states are more qualified to comment on the "China Threat" because of their geographical proximity and relatively smaller size (thus they should be more vulnerable and sensitive), yet it is exactly in these countries that the "China threat" theory is losing its audience. On the contrary, as the global hegemon, the U.S. tends to exaggerate other countries' capability and hostility (it did so versus the Soviet Union and Japan),and China should pay less attention to rhetoric about the "China Threat" coming out from the United States. This, in turn, causes many to argue that China should pay more attention to working with regional states and putting the region in good order rather than to appeasing the "Blue Team" in the U.S. The rationale is that as long as regional states do not take China as a clear and present danger, and China and regional states can manage the region well, it will be hard-pressed for U.S. to forge a coalition of hard-containment. This means that regional states are becoming more important to China, and the weight of U.S. in China's strategic calculus may face a reevaluation.

With the U.S. taking active measures to hedge or even contain China's rise, and China getting less attentive to U.S. concerns when it believes it is acting together with regional states, adding the mutual suspicion already between them, you have a classic security dilemma in the making. This will add yet another dimension of uncertainty to the bilateral relations.

At this juncture, it may be helpful to bring the old "engagement" versus "containment" debate back to the picture. As we understand it, the central purpose for the U.S. and China to engage each other is to gauge each other's intention. Since China is in no position to challenge American global or regional hegemony any time soon, engagement will give the two counties a window of opportunity to feel out each other's intentions and negotiate some sort of peaceful co-existence in the region. However, engagement will fail if: (1) the U.S. is determined to take China's economic growth as essentially threatening, and/or (2) China is determined to expel the U.S. from the Asian region. Under either condition, the possibility for a negotiated peaceful co-existence will be very low. To achieve a negotiated peaceful co-existence, we need more mutual assurance between U.S. and China.

As many have argued, China's current grand strategy and regional strategy does not have much of an element of pushing the U.S. out of Asia, not only because China lacks the capacity but also because China does not deem this to be in its own or the region's interest. Chinese leaders now appreciate some of the constructive roles played by the U.S. in the region are indeed irreplaceable. This recognition has led China to repeatedly assure U.S. that China does not want to expel the U.S. out and China seeks constructive U.S. presence in the region. All these moves signal China's commitment to engagement. The picture from Washington is less clear. Despite the recent warming of relationship and a few U.S. signals of assurance (especially on Taiwan), China is concerned about the possibility that those measures designed to contain China (outlined in the Pentagon's *Quadrennial Defence Review*, but put on hold because of September 11) will be resurrected when Washington finishes its business in Afghanistan and Iraq.

The solution may be that if the U.S. is serious about its engagement policy with China, then it must be ready to assure China that a certain increase of China's influence in the region needs not to be threatening, but actually desirable for long-term U.S. interests, as long as China plays according to international and regional norms, and its influence is channeled through and within regional multilateral initiatives. Indeed, if China is more integrated into the region, it can become a pillar for long-term regional stability; and that outcome will serve long-term U.S. interest far better than a China remaining a regional outcast can (remember North Korea?). After all, isn't this logic the whole logic behind engaging China?

Moreover, the approach may actually gain U.S. more respect (thus influence) in the region, because while regional states do want the U.S. to stay engaged in the region, neither do they want an unwarranted confrontation between U.S. and China because of an active containment (or con-gagement) policy pursued by Washington.

The above solution may well demand a few fundamental changes in the American mentality, and Washington will have to do away with several its self-propagated myths: (1) because the U.S. is the "indispensable nation," it has to lead all regional initiatives all the time; (2) that China wants to push U.S. out of the region and reestablish the "Middle Kingdom Order" in East Asia; and (3) that a divided East Asia is in core U.S. interests.

3

The China-India Border Dispute

The entire China-India boundary has never been formally delimited by any mutually-accepted treaty. There has existed a boundary line of actual control between the two countries. It took shape on the basis of the extent of each other's administrative jurisdiction over a long course of time. The entire boundary has been traditionally divided into three sectors—the eastern sector, the middle sector, and the western sector with all in dispute. The western sector involves the dispute over the Aksai Chin area India claims as part of Latah andChina claims as part of Xinjiang. The middle sector involves a dispute over various points between the Tibet-Kashmir- Punjab border junction and the Nepal-Tibet-Uttar Pradesh border junction. The eastern sector involves a dispute over the area between the pre-1914 Outer Line and the McMahon Line.

In the eastern sector, the British–Indian government had observed the foothills of the Himalayas as the "Outer Line" of its administrative jurisdiction by 1914. Although the Chinese-Tibetan authorities had claimed the tribal areas beyond the British Outer Line within the Tibetan jurisdiction, their administrative jurisdiction actually covered only Tawang tract, the Walong area along the Lohit valley, and some other scattered enclaves in the tribal areas.

Today the line of actual control observed by both sides conforms to the McMahon Line. The disputed area between the pre-1914 Outer Line and the McMahon Line covers a total area of 90,000 square kilometers. According to China, this area is composed of Tibet's three districts of Monyul, Loyul and lower Zayul. According to India, this area is its Arunachal Pradesh, formerly the North-East Frontier Agency of Assam State.

In the western sector, the line of actual control runs roughly along the Karakoram range, conforming to the Chinese claim. The Indian government claims that the boundary runs along the Kunlun range from theKarakoram Pass. The disputed Area is the Aksai Chin region between the two ranges, covering a total area of about 33,000 square kilometers. This area falls mainly in China's Xinjiang and part of it belongs to the Ari District of Tibet. India claims that it is part of its Ladakh area of the State of Jammu and Kashmir. This area, sparsely inhabited, serves as the traffic artery linking Xinjiang and Tibet.

Therefore, in terms of the general China-India border dispute, the McMahon Line in the eastern sector and Aksai Chin in the western sector have been central to the negotiations on the settlement of the border dispute.

The Mystery of the McMahan Line

After Russia successfully divided Mongolia into Outer and Inner Mogolia with the Outer Mongolia as a buffer zone between China and Russia, the British- Indian authorities dreamed the same dream and tried to divideTibet into Outer Tibet and Inner Tibet and made the Outer Tibet as a buffer zone between British India andChina. To achieve such a objective, the Simla conference was held in 1914,with British Henry McMahon, Chinese Chen Ivan, and Tibetan Lonchen shatra as representatives.

There were actually two parallel conferences at Simla, the tripartite conference focusing on the division ofTibet, and the other was the secret one, keeping Chen Ivan out of their negotiations on the Indian-Tibetan boundary. In early 1914, Henry McMahon and Lonchen Shatra secretly negotiated on the division of Tibet and the boundary between Assam and

Tibet as a package deal. An agreement was reached through a secret exchange of notes in Delhi on March 24 and 25, 1914. This boundary line, later known as the McMahon line, was shown on a map in two sheets.

The tripartite conference focused on McMahon's proposal referring to China's suzerainty over Tibet and the outer-inner division of Tibet. On the map attached to the draft convention of the conference, two lines were drawn, one red and the other blue. The red line showed Tibet as a geographical and political unit, and the blue line divided Inner from Outer Tibet. In its southern extension, the red line curves around along the crest of theHimalayas, roughly conforming to the McMahon Line except in the Tawang tract where the McMahon Line reached short of the Tawang tract, implying that the Tawang tract remained part of Tibetan territory. On this map, the Tawang tract was not put within the British-Indian territory.

Without the consent of the Chinese government, Chen Ivan, under McMahon's threat and pressure, initiated the draft convention on April 27, 1914, but with the clear understanding that "to initial and to sign are two different actions," and that his initials would not bind his government, whose views he would immediately seek. The next day, the Chinese government instructed Chen Ivan that "The Chinese representative was forced to initial the draft convention. The Chinese government cannot accept it. You should declare it invalid." Since Chen Ivan refused to sign the draft convention, it was then amended and initialed by McMahon and Lonchen Shatra on July 3, 1914. On the map attached to the draft convention, the McMahon Line was marked just across the town of Tawang, indicating that the area to the north of Tawang would fall within the Tibetan territory.

The British-Indian government did not accept the Simla convention. Viceroy Hardinge forwarded McMahon's report on the Simla conference to London on July 23, 1914, stating that the Indian government recognized that a consideration of the northeastern frontier did not form part of the functions of the conference, and the views and proposal put forward might be regarded as personal to Henry McMahon, not carrying the endorsement of the Government of India. Chen was also instructed to declare that the Chinese government "would not recognize any treaty or similar document that might now or hereafter be signed between Great Britain and Tibet." The Tibetan authorities understood that without securing the Sino-Tibetan boundary, they could not accept the Indo-Tibetan boundary.

The Dalai Lama even recognized the logic relationship between the status of Tibet and the legality of the McMahon Line. In his 1959 address to the Indian Council of World Affairs, he contended that if Tibet had no sovereignty when the Simla convention laid down the McMahon Line, that line was invalid. He challenged Nehru that if you deny the sovereign status to Tibet, you deny the validity of the McMahon Line."

Three maps are related to the Simla conference. One is attached to the March 24 notes; one to the April 27 convention, and the third to the July 3 convention. As far as the Tawang Tract is concerned, the three maps show the McMahon line quite differently. On the first map, the McMahon Line was shown running alng south of the Thagla range far north of Tawang; on the second map, it is not shown in the Tawang tract; and on the third one, it is superimposed on the word " Tawang".

In 1936, Basil Gould, Political Officer in Sikkim, was dispatched to Lhasa and discussed the Tawang issue with the Tibetan government. The Tibetan attitude was Tawang had been Tibetan up to 1914 and they regarded the adjustment of the Tibet-Indian boundary as part and parcel of the general adjustment and determination of boundaries contemplated in the 1914 convention. If they could, with British help, secure a definite Sino-Tibetan boundary, they would observe the Indo-Tibetan border as defined in 1914.

In 1944, just before the British quit from India, basil Gould informed the Tibetan authorities that the Bitish-Indian government was willing to modify the McMahon Line soas to exclude Tawang from the territory it claimed.

He also proposed that the Se La range should be a new boundary line. However, The Tibetan authorities did not accepted it and continued to collect revenues in the Tawang tract and remained administrative control over the Tawang tract. It was in February1951 that the Indian government took over the Tawang tract by force before the PLA entered and liberated Tibet. The Tibetan authorities organized protest demonstrations in Tawang and Lhasaagainst India's occupation of the Tawang tract, but no avail.

As far as the objective of the Simla conference was concerned, it certainly aborted. The McMahon Line was not even accepted by the British-Indian government. After the Simla conference, from 1914 to 1935, on the official maps published by the Survey of India, the McMahon Line was not shown, but instead the Outer Line along the foothills of the Himalayas was shown.

The Tibetan authorities continued to exercise administrative jurisdiction in the tribal areas as they did before.

The Simla conference went down in history as an unaccomplished cause. As to the Simla conference, the first official record appeared in Volume XIV of the 1929 edition of Aichison's Treaties. It did not refer to the McMahon Line, but to the discussion on the Sino-Tibetan frontier. It was stated that a tripartite convention was drawn up and initialed in 1914, but the Chinese government refused to permit its representative to proceed to full signature.

In 1935, Olaf Caroe, deputy secretary of the Foreign and Political Department of the British-Indian Government discovered the secret documents of the Simla conference in dealing with a case involving the illegal entry into Tibet through the Tawang tract. He realized that the northeastern frontier might be a matter of dispute with the Chinese in the future. He proposed to revise the official record of the Simla conference in the Aichison's Treaties and show the McMahon Line on the official maps. The British government approved his proposal.

This original 1929 edition was soon withdrawn from circulation and replaced by a spurious edition, actually printed in 1938, but with an imprint of 1929. However, at least three copies of the original 1929 edition survived, one in Peking Library, one in Harvard University library, and one in the India Office. In the revised edition, it was stated that the Simla conference negotiated an agreement on the status of Tibet and the boundary of Tibet with both China and India. Such a revision was nothing but scandalous diplomatic forgery. Then the McMahon Line began to appear of the Indian official maps. However, it was still marked as "Undemarcated Boundary."

CHINA'S CLAIM TO TIBET IS FACTOR IN BORDER DISPUTE

This is perhaps the most militarized Buddhist enclave in the world. Perched above 10,000 feet in the icy reaches of the eastern Himalayas, the town of Tawang is not only home to one of Tibetan Buddhism's most sacred monasteries but also the site of a massive Indian military buildup. Convoys of army trucks haul howitzers along rutted mountain roads. Soldiers drill in muddy fields. Military bases appear every half-mile in the countryside, with watchtowers rising behind concertina wire.

A road sign on the northern edge of town helps explain the reason for all the fear and the fury: The border with China is just 23 miles away; Lhasa, the Tibetan capital, 316 miles; and Beijing 2,676 miles. "The Chinese army has a big deployment at the border, at Bumla," said Madan Singh, a junior commissioned officer who sat with a half-dozen soldiers one afternoon sipping tea beside a fog-cloaked road. "That's why we're here." Though little known to the outside world, Tawang is a flashpoint in relations between the world's two most populous nations. It is the focus of China's most delicate land-border dispute, a conflict rooted in Chinese claims of sovereignty over all of historical Tibet.

In recent months, both countries have stepped up efforts to secure their rights over this rugged patch of land. China tried to block a \$2.9 billion loan to India from the Asian Development Bank on the grounds that part of the loan was slated for water projects in Arunachal Pradesh, the state that includes Tawang. It was the first time China had sought to influence the territorial dispute through a multilateral institution. Then an Indian general announced that the Indian military was deploying extra troops and fighter jets in the area. The growing belligerence has soured relations between the two Asian giants and has prompted one Indian military leader to declare that China has replaced Pakistan as India's biggest threat.

Economic progress might be expected to bring the countries closer. China and India did $52 billion of trade last year, a 34 percent increase over 2007. But businesspeople say that border tensions have infused official deliberations over business deals, dampening the willingness of Chinese and Indian companies to invest in each other's countries. "Officials start taking more time, scrutinizing things more carefully, and all that means more delays and ultimately more denials," said Ravi Bhoothalingam, a former president of the Oberoi Group, the luxury hotel chain, and a member of the Institute of Chinese Studies in New Delhi. "That's not good for business."

The roots of the conflict go back to China's territorial claims to Tibet. Not only does the Dalai Lama, the exiled spiritual leader of the Tibetans, live in the foothills of the western Himalayas with the blessing of the Indian government, but China insists that this swath of northeast India has historically been part of Tibet, and thus should be part of China. Tawang is a thickly forested area of white stupas and steep, terraced hillsides that is home to the ethnic Monpa people, who practice Tibetan Buddhism, speak a language similar to Tibetan and once paid tribute to rulers in Lhasa. The 6th Dalai Lama was born here in the 17th century.

The Chinese army occupied Tawang briefly in 1962, during a war with India fought over this and other territories along the 2,521-mile border. More than 3,100 Indian soldiers and 700 Chinese soldiers were killed and thousands wounded in the border war. War memorials highlighting China's aggressions in Tawang here are big draws for Indian tourists. "The entire border is disputed," said Ma Jiali, an India scholar at the China Institutes of Contemporary International Relations, a government-supported think tank in Beijing. "This problem hasn't been solved, and it's a huge barrier to China-India relations."

In some ways, Tawang has become a proxy battleground, too, between China and the Dalai Lama, who passed through this valley when he fled into exile in 1959. From his home in the distant hill town of Dharamsala, he wields enormous influence over Tawang. He appoints the abbot of the powerful monastery and gives financial support to institutions throughout the area. Last year, the Dalai Lama announced for the first time that Tawang is a part of India, bolstering the Indian government's territorial claims and infuriating China.

Traditional Tibetan culture runs strong in Tawang. At the Tawang monastery, an important centre of Tibetan learning, monks express apprehension about China's rule over Tibet, which the Chinese army seized in 1951.

"I hate the Chinese government," said Gombu Tsering, 70, a senior monk who watches over the monastery's museum. "Tibet wasn't even a part of China.

Lhasa wasn't a part of China." Few expect China to try to forcefully annex Tawang, but military skirmishes are a real danger, analysts say. The Indian military recorded 270 border violations and nearly 2,300 instances of "aggressive border patrolling" by Chinese soldiers last year, said Brahma Chellaney, a professor of strategic studies at the Centre for Policy Research, a research organization in New Delhi. Mr. Chellaney has advised the Indian government's National Security Council.

"The India-China frontier has become more 'hot' than the India-Pakistan border," he said in an e-mail. China has grown increasingly hostile to the Dalai Lama after a severe outbreak of ethnic unrest in Tibet. This year, it turned its diplomatic guns on India. China moved in March to block a $2.9 billion loan to India from the Asian Development Bank, a multi-nation group based in Manila that has China on its board, because $60 million of the loan had been earmarked for flood-control projects in Arunachal Pradesh, the state that includes Tawang. The loan was approved in mid-June over China's heated objections.

Weeks after China first tried to block the loan, the chief of the Indian air force, now retired, told a prominent Indian newspaper that China posed a greater threat than Pakistan. Another official, J.J. Singh, the governor of Arunachal Pradesh and retired chief of the Indian army, said the next month that the Indian military was adding two divisions of troops, totalling 50,000 to 60,000 soldiers, to the border region over the next several years.

Four Sukhoi fighter jets were immediately deployed to a nearby air base. Since 2005, when Chinese Prime Minister Wen Jiabao visited India, the two countries have gone through 13 rounds of bilateral negotiations over the issue. A last round was just held last month, with no results. Though China has actually resolved many of its border disputes in recent years, India remains a glaring exception.

The Government of Tibet in Exile

From July 20 to 23, 1994, Beijing staged the Third Forum on Work in Tibet which recommended the total destruction of an entire civilization flourishing on the Tibetan Plateau for thousands of years. This cultural "empire" once encompassed far-flung areas like Buryatia, Tuva and Kalmykia in Russia; Mongolia; Laddakh, Lahaul-Spiti, Sikkim, and Arunachal Pradesh in India; Mustang, Dolpo and Solō Khumbu in Nepal; Bhutan and parts of western China.

The policy formulated in 1994 in Beijing-and these days pursued with Cultural Revolutionary zeal in Tibet-will mean the annihilation of the spiritual homeland of this shared culture. Implementation of the Third Work Forum is thus having a crippling impact on the traditional culture of millions of non-Tibetans as the well-spring of their cultural inspiration is forcibly drained and there is nothing to replenish the continuous growth and development of this distinct and highly evolved civilization.

Losing Hearts and Minds

The decisions made at the Third Forum rest on two fundamental conclusions which Beijing drew. It realized it was losing out in two vital fields-ideology and propaganda. For a state whose existence is justified by its ideological superiority and the power of its propaganda to shape the thinking of the masses, the implications of this for the future was at best uncertain, at worst dangerous. Beijing concluded it was losing the ideological war because, despite the unrelenting assault on Tibetan Buddhism, Tibetans were as devoted to their traditional beliefs as ever. Beijing has succeeded in physically enslaving the country but it has not won over the hearts, minds and loyalty of the Tibetan populace.

Communist ideology, enforced by the military might of China, had failed to dent the heart of Buddhism. Added to this was the communist authorities' total bafflement at the non-violent policy underpinning the Middle Way Approach advocated by His Holiness the Dalai Lama to resolve the issue of Tibet's future status. For a regime which is based on Mao's dictum that political power grows out of the barrel of a gun, this supposedly eccentric philosophy which says victory lies in capturing the hearts and minds of people by the power of ideas rather than killing by the power of the gun comes as a bolt from the blue. Much of Beijing's knee-jerk reaction to, and its bafflement at, His Holiness the Dalai Lama's new policy of rapprochement lies at the heart of its new hardline policy.

Beijing considered it was losing the propaganda war because, for one reason or the other, the world's media and its pop culture considered-at least for the moment-Tibet and Tibetan Buddhism their very own cuddly pandas. Despite its financial might China found it extremely difficult to exterminate this image of Tibet and get its voice heard on the Tibetan issue in the court of the international media. In order to address these weaknesses the Third Forum concentrated on two issues. One was to focus on Tibet's economic development in the hope that this would keep Tibetan demonstrations off the streets. This was tantamount to bribing the Tibetans with promises of riches to come if they toed the party line. The other concern was to win the coming and new generations of Tibetans over to the Chinese viewpoint.

Beijing has given up on the present generation of Tibetans as a lost cause. If the coming generations of Tibetans were also lost to the 'Dalai Clique' this, the Chinese concluded, would have dangerous consequences for Chinese rule in Tibet. The 15-year-old Gyalwa Karmapa's dramatic escape from Tibet in January 2000 was a warning to the Beijing authorities of the erosion of loyalty to China. The Karmapa's flight, and the earlier escape of Agya Rinpoche, the abbot of Kumbum Monastery, came as a huge embarrassment for China, because retaining these high lamas gave China a degree of legitimacy for its rule in Tibet. This is the reason why Beijing is enforcing with greater strictness its 1993 instruction of recalling young Tibetans studying in schools and monasteries run by Dharmasala in India. This is also the rationale for Beijing closing down schools in Tibet which are privately run by Tibetans.

For these reasons Tibet today is in the throes of a second Cultural Revolution as the Chinese authorities step up their long-term strategy to exterminate Tibet's distinct cultural and ethnic identity. The authorities are pursuing a four-pronged strategy to achieve their final objective. They have stepped up repression while employing their huge propaganda machine to paint a rosy picture of Tibet. They have quickened the pace of economic development to dampen Tibetan nationalism and are simultaneously moving more Chinese settlers onto the Tibetan Plateau to change Tibet's demographic composition and to ease social unrest because of mounting unemployment back in China.

The Third Work Forum on Tibet was convened by the top Chinese leadership and was presided over by President Jiang Zemin. The authorities have now enshrined this Work Forum as the most "important strategic policy to rejuvenate Tibet" and have hailed its directives as the new manifesto for party work on the plateau. The significance of the Third Work Forum lies in the fact that it overturned the more liberal policies laid out for Tibet's "development" by the First and Second Work Forums held in 1980 and 1984.

The first two work forums were initiated by the late Hu Yaobang, then Secretary General of the Chinese Communist Party. This liberal and somewhat maverick leader is credited with masterminding a series of measures to improve the social, economic and political conditions in Tibet. The brief spell of liberalization markedly improved the living conditions of the majority of Tibetans and contributed to a more relaxed intellectual and social climate.

The Third Work Forum reversed these policies and reinstated hardline measures under which Tibet is still reeling today. The Tibetans in Tibet perceive the current repressive policies as a second Cultural Revolution. The question is why did China choose to jettison its earlier more liberal policies and adopt a manifesto which is leading to the systematic destruction of Tibet's distinct culture. The answer lies in domestic and international events which forced China to formulate a series of hardline policies on Tibet which eventually crystallized into the Third Work Forum for Tibet. The world which confronted China in the late 1980s and early 1990s was a frightening one.

Starting from 1987, Tibet was rocked by a string of protest demonstrations, which called for Tibetan independence. One of the largest demonstrations which erupted on March 5, 1989 in Lhasa, forced the authorities to impose martial law on the city. These demonstrations are now seen to have been an inspiration behind the outburst of Chinese students' pro-democracy uprisings. The authorities saw the series of Tiananmen Square demonstrations as a sign of their Central Government losing control, and in an attempt to regain supremacy, the authorities slaughtered-perhaps hundreds if not thousands of students on June 4, 1989. These demonstrations were a chilling replay to the authorities of the May 4, 1919 student demonstrations in Beijing which signalled a political and cultural awakening across the erstwhile Middle Kingdom.

Bejing's fears of losing control were exacerbated by external events which saw the unraveling of the communist world. The

Solidarity Movement in Poland, the fall of the Berlin Wall, and the implosion of the Soviet Union fed Beijing's paranoia over threats to the Chinese Communist Party hold on power. Official China's fears were further inflamed by the rapidly changing attitude of the broad masses as they turned back from communism to traditional beliefs like Confucionism, Buddhism, Islam, Christianity and indigenous folk cults. In the eyes of ordinary citizens communism was becoming totally discredited and this, more than anything else, was the biggest nightmare for China's leadership. The leadership's justification for staying in power was being disavowed by the masses. For a one-party dictatorship this historically indicates the first step along the slippery road to dissolution and removal of power.

For these reasons the Chinese leadership then reverted to its earlier view that traditional beliefs were its real enemy. In competing with Buddhism, Confucionism, Islam, Christianity and other isms, communism was losing out in terms of its ability to retain the loyalty and allegiance of the masses. The leadership revived the old aphorisms once served up to the Tibetan people to justify their policies to destroy Tibetan Buddhism during the Cultural Revolution. Bewildered Tibetans were then told that just as there cannot be two suns in the sky, so there cannot be both Buddhism and socialism in Tibet. Inevitably Buddhism then had to give way to socialism. And again, today, religion is being blatantly sublimated to Chinese state power.

These were the fears of the Chinese leaders when they met in Beijing in 1994 to hammer out their new Tibet initiatives. For the Chinese authorities Tibet is an especially sensitive issue because of their conviction that hostile Western forces are using the issue of Tibet to "westernize" China and to lead to its territorial fragmentation. The third generation Chinese leaders came to the conclusion that stability in Tibet was vital to the stability of China as a whole. Earlier, Tibet was merely of peripheral concern to the vital interests of China's sprawling communist empire. Now, with the Third Work Forum, the authorities were saying, "We must clearly understand that we must do our work in Tibet not only for the sake our of own region's stability and development, not only for the interests of our people, but also for the sake of the whole nation's stability and development."

In Tibet, China faced peculiar problems because of the inherent strength of Tibetan Buddhism and the depth of devotion of the populace to His Holiness the Dalai Lama. The sustained burst of religious revival that followed in the wake of the brief spell of liberalization in Tibet confirmed the leadership's worst fears that decades of concerted assault on Tibetan culture and religion had not extinguished the people's traditional beliefs and values. From merely nuisance value, the Chinese leadership now viewed Tibetan Buddhism as a very real and imminent threat to the stability of Chinese rule in Tibet.

At the same time the Chinese leadership's attitude towards His Holiness the Dalai Lama changed. From being an uncertain ally in the peace process in Tibet, the current Chinese leadership now saw him as a full-blown "enemy". A top-level conclave held in Beijing on March 10, 1993 concluded that, "There are different factions within the Dalai Clique; they are, however, unanimous in their political nature and position. They differ from each other in ideological viewpoints and ways of expressing them. Different strategies must be adopted to use their differences, to deal with them differently in order to divide and destroy them."

Repeated statements by high-level officials describe the struggle against "splittism", the official term for Tibetan independence, as a "life-and-death struggle". At the 1994 annual meeting of the "TAR" Communist Party Committee to brief members on the policy thrust of the Third Work Forum on Tibet, Raidi, deputy Secretary of the Committee said, "Up to now, his (the Dalai Lama's) standpoint on Tibet's independence has never changed, and we must reveal his double-faced true colour. The focal point in our region in the struggle against splittism is to oppose the Dalai Clique. As the saying goes, to kill a serpent, one must first cut off its head."

In short, the Third Work Forum decided that Beijing was in a position to solve the Tibet issue without the Dalai Lama's involvement. It abandoned the earlier liberal policy of including His Holiness the Dalai Lama in any future settlement of Tibet's status. His Holiness the Dalai Lama was clearly singled out as the cause of China's "Tibet problem".

The Third Work Forum also abandoned the policy of granting concessions to Tibet because of the plateau's "special characteristics". This policy had been the cornerstone of recommendations made by the First and Second Tibet Work Forums.

To carry out its new hardline policies in Tibet, Beijing appointed Chen Kuiyuan as the "TAR" Party Secretary in 1992. Chen Kuiyuan's appointment is significant because he had a track record for being a tough and ruthless administrator. He had already served as the First Secretary of the Chinese Communist Party in Inner Mongolia and is credited with repressing the rebellious Mongols, many of whom refer to him as "the butcher". Chen Kuiyuan was especially recommended to the post by Hu Jintao, the current Vice-President of China, who was then the First Secretary of the Chinese Communist Party in Tibet.

Tackling Tibetan Nationalism

The Third Work Forum policies chalked out for Tibet contained four key elements. China stepped up the scale of repression in Tibet. External propaganda work was escalated. The pace of economic development in Tibet-and its corollary of encouraging more Chinese settlers and businessmen to take advantage of the economic boom on the "roof of the world"-was also increased. In short, Beijing had decided to tackle Tibetan nationalism head-on and observers are still assessing the consequences on both Chinese rule in Tibet and on the populace.

Beijing remains convinced that these key components of its current policy will stabilize Chinese rule over Tibet and solve once and for all, the vexed problem of its negative image over the way Tibet has been handled. One main target of the current policy of repression is Tibetan Buddhism. Chinese leaders are increasingly alarmed by the proliferation of monasteries and temples which the period of liberalization spawned throughout Tibet: they are seen as the bastions of Tibetan nationalism. The authorities have set up "Democratic Management Committees" to control monasteries and nunneries and created "Work Inspection Teams" to supervise the "education" of monks and nuns.

A major thrust is underway to break the bond of loyalty between the clergy in Tibet and His Holiness the Dalai Lama in India. Campaigns like "Strike Hard" and "Patriotic Re-education", unleashed in 1996, are aimed at crippling the rise of Tibetan Buddhism which the authorities suspect is weaning the loyalty of the Tibetan people away from the communist party and towards His Holiness the Dalai Lama.

One salient feature of the "Strike Hard" campaign is how differently it is interpreted in China and Tibet. China's "Strike Hard" campaign was started to weed out corruption. Tibet's version is used as a political tool to eliminate those whom the authorities label "splittists". In Tibet, rather than striking at corruption, the authorities turn a blind eye to this social disease in the hope that it will erode the traditional morality of Tibetans and undermine Tibetan Buddhism.

In fact, at a secret meeting held in December 1999 in Chengdu, capital of Sichuan province, Chen Kuiyuan, the hardline Party Secretary of "TAR" recommended to the Central Chinese Government that an all-out effort must be made to eradicate Tibetan Buddhism and culture from the face of the earth so that no memory of them will be left in the minds of coming generations of Tibetans-except as museum pieces.

Chen Kuiyuan stated that the main cause of instability is the existence of the Dalai Lama and his Government-in-Exile in Dharamsala and these must be "uprooted". He recommended that Tibet, Tibetan people and Tibetan Buddhism-in other words the very name of Tibet-must be destroyed and the "Tibet Autonomous Region" be merged with provinces like Sichuan. While treating Tibetans to boot-heel subjugation at home, internationally China was on an overdrive propaganda blitz.

At a brainstorming conclave held on March 10, 1993, Zeng Jian-hui, Vice-Minister of the Propaganda Ministry, told participants, "The propaganda work on the question of Tibet is one of the focal points of the entire external propaganda work...With regard to attacks by the West and the Dalai Clique and their frequent activities, our external propaganda should launch offensive.

We should expand our spheres of influence; in particular, we should infiltrate our propaganda into the mainstream life of the West.

"Firstly we should continue to send Tibetan scholars and Tibetan singing and dancing troupes abroad to lecture and perform. Secondly, relevant embassies and consulates should aim at the public opinion and the activities of the Dalai Clique in the countries where they are stationed and utilize speeches, picture exhibitions, special articles and other forms to carry out propaganda work, so as to win over officials and people of those countries... We should reinforce the work of utilizing the power of foreign propaganda. A few years ago, in the light of the situation of that time, we made arrangements for foreign journalists to visit Tibet."

The September 3, 2000 edition of *People's Daily* carried a story headlined "Tibet Welcomes Foreign Journalists for Objective Reporting". It stated that "A senior Tibetan official said Sunday that Tibet welcomes foreign journalists to come for objective and just reporting, but not those who take distorted views. Raidi, Deputy Secretary of the Tibet Autonomous Regional Committee of the Communist Party of China and Chairman of the Standing Committee of the Tibetan Autonomous Regional People's Congress, made the remarks at a meeting here with a press delegation of Thailand." In this context, it is interesting to note that N. Ram, the editor of

India's *Frontline* magazine, devoted 36 pages of the September 15, 2000 issue to promote the Chinese line and recommended that the Indian Government expel the Central Tibetan Administration from Indian soil for being the main stumbling block to normal relations between India and China. It is difficult to assess to what extent the views contained in his stupendous reporting marathon are his own.

These editorial outbursts are in line with policy decisions outlined in the early nineties. During a two-day secret conclave in March 1993 in Chengdu, Vice-Minister Zeng Jian-hui, told participants, "All foreigners that we entertain and send to Tibet must have a relatively objective opinion of Tibet. We should use people from abroad to carry out the propaganda on Tibet for us, which is more powerful than if we do it."

Along with its external public relations strategy, China is presently carrying out a potentially much more dangerous policy of speeding up the pace of Tibet's economic development and its related drive to bring more Chinese settlers onto the Tibetan Plateau. Beijing's Western China Development Programme, which incorporates Tibet in its ambit, is devised to shift the focus of China's economic activities from Coastal China to the interior-both to narrow the imbalance in the level of economic development between the two regions and to ease population pressure on the coastal areas which attract millions of migrant workers.

The focus of Beijing's Western China Economic Development Programme in Tibet is to exploit the plateau's still untapped minerals and other natural resources and to upgrade Tibet's infrastructure-like roads and telecommunications-to facilitate transportation of these resources to China. The other purpose of the heightened level of economic activity is to divert the Tibetans' attention from their political fate to focus on their livelihood-thus undermining Tibetan nationalism. The Chinese authorities aim to manipulate the situation in Tibet still further by bringing in more Chinese settlers who would then demographically cement Chinese rule once and for all. These current hardline policies and their implementation in Tibet are impacting the stalled Sino-Tibetan Dialogue and will vitally affect the ability of Tibetans to survive as a distinct people and culture.

Beijing's Flawed Perceptions

The basic flaws in China's new policy in its search to resolve the problem of Tibet is thinking the solution can exclude the involvement of His Holiness the Dalai Lama. The other is in attempting to solve the problem over the heads of Tibet's citizens.

These two fundamental mistakes will exacerbate China's Tibet problem, not solve it. The reason lies in the history of Tibet and in the sentiments of the people. The institution of the Dalai Lamas of Tibet is more than 600 years old, if we start from the birth of the first Dalai Lama in 1391. In the course of its growth and development, the very institution itself came to symbolize fundamental beliefs and the political destiny of the nation. The bond between the Dalai Lamas and the Tibetan people is fundamental and unbreakable; any attempt, however sustained, will never succeed in driving a wedge between the two.

Consequently, China's current policy of forcing Tibetans-especially monks and nuns-to denounce His Holiness the Dalai Lama and pledge loyalty to the Chinese Communist Party will prove counterproductive. In view of this the Third Work Forum's basic assumption that in the case of Tibet time is on the side of China, and that Beijing can stall the problem of Tibet till the demise of the present Dalai Lama whereupon the issue of Tibet will solve itself, is fatally flawed-based as it is on a mistaken perception of the role played by the institution of the Dalai Lamas in the development of Tibetan history.

This assumption, if not reviewed, revised and abandoned, will prove catastrophic for the Chinese leadership and for those who chose to turn their whimsical personal analysis into state policy. The reason is simple. The Chinese Communist Party was founded in the 1920s and came to power in 1949. Within this short span of time the masses have lost faith in communist ideology, and members of the party these days pay mere lip service to the ideological justifications of the party. Conversely, the institution of the Dalai Lamas as a political force is more than 300 years old.

These days the Dalai Lama is recognized by Tibetans throughout the world as the heart of Tibetan nationalism. How can a party which has lost its soul outlast an institution which symbolizes the very soul of a people? For these reasons it is imperative for China to review and re-assess its current hardline stance towards Tibet. China must re-start its stalled peace process over Tibet and consider His Holiness the Dalai Lama as a vital and active partner in the procedures. If China does this it will have won a powerful ally and companion along the road to peace, stability and continued prosperity.

4

Sino-Indian Territorial Problems

In terms of "the rise of China" and its "implications for India", the title of this book, the Sino-Indian territorial dispute represents an immediate arena in which India is having to face the uncomfortable implications from having an increasingly stronger neighbour. For India, the ability of China to deny India's hopes of territorial settlement on India's terms has become ever clearer in the wake of China's rise in military power in and around their disputed territory, which remains the biggest amount of land still in dispute in Asia.

As such, "the 4,056—kilometre (2,520 miles) frontier between India and China, one of the longest inter-state borders in the world, remains ... not defined, let alone demarcated, on maps or delineated on the ground". Here, the judgement over a century ago of Lord Curzon, British Viceroy of India 1898-1905 still seems relevant; the most urgent work of Foreign Ministers and Ambassadors ... is now the conclusion of Frontier Conventions in which sources of discord are removed by the adjustment of rival interests or ambitions at points where the territorial borders adjoin", for "frontiers are indeed the razor's edge on which hang suspended the modern issues of war or peace, of life or death to nations". Admittedly, the territorial issue has been officially decoupled from the wider Sino-Indian relationship; as with the PRC rhetoric that "China and India have already reached consensus on the border issue. Before it is completely resolved, both countries will endeavour to maintain peace and stability in the border areas and will not let the border issue affect the general picture of China and India's cooperation". However, in reality their territorial issues do affect their wider relationship, in PRC terms "the existence of immense territorial disputes between China and India".

In dispute terms, this chapter argues that, in International Relations (IR) theory terms, the territorial disputes between India and China involve *classical geopolitics* entwined with *critical geopolitics*. Each strand of geopolitics, in their different ways, both involve the respective "position" that India and China hold for themselves and for each other in their immediate and extended neighbourhood. Whilst each side argues from history, the chapter argues that in reality the evidence from history is rather ambiguous and inconclusive for both sides' territorial claims. Indeed, history is a sterile area to argue from, as one Indian commentator put it, "can we go beyond history to look at solutions which do not hark back to the past?" The chapter argues that, from the outside, resolution of the issue seems feasible enough in terms of simple seeming territorial trade offs involving Arunachal Pradesh and Aksai Chin; but is complicated by smaller geographic issues surrounding Tawang, and wider geopolitical issues surrounding Tibet and indeed the balance of power in Asia between India and China.

The two main areas of dispute along this Himalayan frontier are the *Western Sector* (Aksai Chin, around 37,250 square kilometres/ 14,380 square miles); and the *Eastern Sector* (Arunachal Pradesh, around 83,740 square kilometres/ 32,330 square miles). On the one hand, Arunachal Pradesh is inhabited by over a million people, Indian citizens, and includes important Buddhist centres like Tawang. On the other hand, Aksai Chin is a virtually uninhabited bleak barren plateau with no permanent settlements. It is the place "where not a blade of grass grows" as Jawaharlal Nehru once dismissively said; but where China's National Highway 219 runs through Aksai Chin as a key geopolitical infrastructure link for the PRC between its provinces of Tibet and Xinjiang. One further complication is China's occupation of the Shaksgam valley; around 5,180 sq kilometres/1,930 square miles, to which Pakistan relinquished its Baltistan-related claims in 1963, but over which India maintains its own Kashmir-derived claims. Smaller pockets of disputed territory are found, the *Middle Sector* fringes of Himachal Pradesh and Uttar Pradesh. Elsewhere along the Himalayas, lingering uncertainty over China's recognition of Sikkim's incorporation into India in 1975 is entwined with continuing PRC claims to the "Finger Area" in the north of Sikkim, with 71 supposed incidents reported of Chinese troop "incursions" in 2008. Nearby territorial disputes between China and Bhutan around the Chumbi Valley triangulation point with India are of further concern to New Delhi, given the Chumbi Valley's location looking down onto the India's sensitive Siliguri corridor which links India's northeastern states with the rest of India.

Wider nuances arise with India's Foreign Secretary (2004—2006) Shyam Saran, and his comments about *the logic of geography*. In front of one audience, it was a question for Saran of "geopolitical reality" in which "I would like to focus particularly on Asia, where the interests of both India and China intersect. It is said that the logic of geography is unrelenting. Proximity is the most difficult and testing among diplomatic challenges a country faces", where "to those who harbour any skepticism about this fact, it would suffice to remind that we share one of the longest [and disputed] land borders in the world with China. In front of another audience, it was again a question that "it is said that the logic of geography is unrelenting and proximity is the most difficult and testing among diplomatic challenges a country faces"; with the following gloss that "frontiers with neighbours are where domestic concerns intersect with external relationships. This is where domestic and foreign policies become inextricable and demand sensitive handling", and in which "it is important for us to look at the [disputed] boundary question from the long-term and strategic perspective of India-China relations, rather than as a mere territorial issue.

The territorial issues between India and China form one of the biggest land disputes in Asia, and are of significance not only for the size of area under dispute, but also because the two disputants are the big countries most evidently on the rise in Asia. Alongside this *logic of geography*, there is then what Neville Maxwell called "the logic of power"; a *logic of power* whereby powerful states "in their expansive phases push out their frontiers until they meet the resistance of a strong neighbour or reach a physical barrier which makes a natural point of rest". In geopolitical terms, the current point of rest is along the Himalayas/Karakoram range, but in the long term where exactly is the "natural" point of rest between them? Amidst talk of mutual IR *security dilemma* dynamics, China's strengthening of military forces and related infrastructure in Aksai Chin and Arunachal Pradesh zones is now a spur to India's own more halting augmentation of military forces and related infrastructure. Meanwhile, both countries are seeking to expand their wider strategic space at a time when their immediate mountain borders remain unresolved.

STATUS OF NEGOTIATIONS

In 1981, following the frozen relations prevalent after the 1962 war, border talks at the vice-ministerial level were initiated. Although Beijing had suggested sectoral swapping in 1960 and 1980, this *overall package* predisposition faced India's push for separate *sector-by-sector* agreements. In 1988 more formal Joint Working Group (JWG) discussions were started; with a twin mandate of ensuring "peace and tranquillity" along the Line of Actual Control (LAC) and working on a "fair, reasonable and mutually acceptable" settlement of the boundary question.

In September 1993, China and India signed the *Agreement on the Maintenance of Peace and Tranquillity along the Line of Actual Control in the India-China Border Areas*, with a Sino-Indian Expert Group (EG) set up to assist the work of the JWG on the boundary question.

The rhetoric was clear in its Article-1; "the India-China boundary question shall be resolved through peaceful and friendly consultations. Neither side shall use or threaten to use force against the other by any means. Pending an ultimate solution to the boundary question...".

In November 1996, China and India agreed in their *Agreement on Confidence Building Measures in the Military Field along the Line of Actual Control in the India-China Border Areas* to delimit their Line of Actual Control (LAC) and institute Confidence Building Measures (CBMs) along the frontier. The agreement included pledges on nonaggression, prior notification of large troop movements, a 10-km no-fly zone for combat aircraft, and exchange of maps to resolve disagreements about the precise location of the LAC.

In June 2003, the India—China *Declaration on Principles for Relations and Comprehensive Cooperation between India and China* had the two countries agreeing "to each appoint a special representative to explore from the political perspective of the overall bilateral relationship the framework of a boundary settlement". Some ground rules for actual territorial negotiations seemed to have been achieved in April 2005 with the signing of the *Political Parameters and Guiding Principles for the Settlement of the India-China Boundary Question*. However, the *Joint Declaration by the Republic of India and the People's Republic of China* (2006) and the *Shared Vision for the 21st Century of the People's Republic of China and the Republic of India* (2008), which both expressed hopes that "such [boundary] differences are not allowed to affect the positive development of bilateral relations" in other fields, have perhaps pushed territorial differences but also territorial resolution to one side?

To conclude, varied frameworks have been seen; some eight rounds of vice-ministerial talks from 1981—1987, fourteen Joint Working Group meetings from 1988—2003, and thirteen rounds of Special Representative talks from 2003—2009. Nevertheless, there seems to have been little substantive progress on territorial issues. Specific discussions on core territorial demands and delineation of forces have given way to broader, but some would say vaguer and less useful, political discussions of bilateral relations as a whole. In terms of general confidence, if anything, the situation has deteriorated between India and China, where the last few years have seen growing numbers of incursions, alongside infrastructure and military forces build up along the Himalayas, both on the Arunachal Pradesh and Aksai Chin borderlines. Despite some of the diplomatic rhetoric of engagement and global cooperation, strategic perceptions of each other have deteriorated, whilst public as well as elite distrust of intentions and military capacity has grown.

Even initial specific steps have been minimal and indeed appear somewhat grudging. In terms of establishing the Lines of Actual Control (LAC), maps have only been established with regard to the relatively minor *Middle Sector* (Himachal Pradesh/ Uttar Pradesh fringes) where LAC maps were exchanged in November 2000. China then committed itself to an exchange of LAC maps of the *Western Sector* in 2002 and the *Eastern Sector* (Arunachal Pradesh) in early 2003. However, in 2003 this was effectively overturned when China argued that the two countries should instead focus on achieving an overall final political package settlement.

Equally well, the 2006 Joint Declaration pledge that "it was agreed to complete the process of exchanging maps indicating their respective perceptions of the entire alignment of the LAC on the basis of already agreed parameters as soon as possible" also has shown no particular signs of being completed; with no LAC maps having emerged for those two major blocks of disputed territory, Aksai Chin and Arunachal Pradesh. This in turn makes the immediate implementation of the 1996 *Agreement on Confidence Building Measures in the Military Field along the Line of Actual Control in the India-China Border Areas* difficult as the agreement refers to controlling military dispositions and deployments to certain distances from Lines of Actual Control, but yet those LACs have not been established.

The speed, or rather lack of speed, over negotiations is noticeable, a "glacial pace" given that current border discussions were first initiated in 1981. The 2005 *Political Parameters and Guiding Principles for the Settlement of the India-China Boundary Question* talked of "an early settlement of the boundary question" It did have its Article-7 provision that "in reaching a boundary settlement, the two sides shall safeguard due interests of their settled populations in the border areas". However, China's strong reassertion of its claims over Arunachal Pradesh, and especially Tawang, cut across such population principles. This population provision also seems undercut by the comments made to Pranab Mukherjee in June 6, 2007 by Chinese Foreign Minister Yang Jiechi, who stated that "mere presence" of settled populations would not affect China's claims. Meanwhile, the 2006 *Joint Declaration* announced that "the Special Representatives shall complete at an early date the task of finalising an appropriate framework for a final package settlement covering all sectors of the India-China boundary", but as of yet there are no signs of any such "early finalisation" let alone "early settlement". Similarly, the *Working Group* set up at the 2007 Special Representatives meeting to prepare a "framework arrangement" has been equally barren on outcomes, so far.

Indian perceptions of Chinese motives remain highly critical. For Kapila it was the opportunity for China "to keep alive the border dispute as a strategic pressure point against India". For Malik it was a case that "Beijing would not want to give up the 'bargaining chip' that an unsettled boundary vis-à-vis India provides it with. An unsettled border provides China the strategic leverage to keep India uncertain about its intentions, and nervous about its capabilities, while exposing India's vulnerabilities and weaknesses, and ensuring New Delhi's 'good behaviour' on issues of vital concern to China".

Discussions, rather than negotiations have then settled down into a regular, but desultory fashion. The press communiqué from the 2009 Special Representative talks was still noticeably bland; "in a friendly and candid atmosphere, the two Special Representatives had an in-depth exchange of views on resolving the boundary question.

Both countries agreed to press ahead with the framework negotiations in accordance with the agreed political parameters and guiding principle", so as "to seek for a fair and reasonable solution acceptable to both. Prior to that, both should work together to maintain peace and tranquillity in the border areas. Candid is often diplomatic euphemism for blunt differences of opinion, whilst the call for working together to maintain peace and tranquillity is a virtual admission that peace and stability has not yet been established. Equally euphemistic are PRC statements that both countries "should respect history and reality, take into account the feelings of both nations, make the most of their political wisdom and come up with a reasonable and mutually acceptable solution to their border issue". Such sentiments fail to give any tangible specifics on what actual solutions might be forthcoming.

DISPUTED TERRITORY BETWEEN CHINA AND INDIA

Arunachal Pradesh

Both countries retain their strong claims to the disputed territory, however, fueled by national pride and national security interests. China's "Go West" development policy and July 2006 opening of the Qinghai-Tibet railway have received mixed responses from Indian policymakers; those who favour expanded trade and people-to-people contacts have regarded the developments as positive, but some within the national security establishment have raised concerns that they will allow Beijing to extend its military power projection into Tibet and beyond into South and Central Asia.

Three rivers running through India—the Indus/Sengge Chu, Sutlej/Langqen Tsangbo, and Brahmaputra/Sang Po—originate in Tibet, a fact that has spurred Indian fears that China could use upstream dams and barrages to control the flow of water into India. India, for instance, has blamed a series of flash floods along the Sutlej River in its state of Himachal Pradesh to China's reluctance to supply hydrological data to India in a timely manner or allow Indian scientists to conduct surveys of melting glaciers on Chinese soil. The absence of any water-sharing treaty between both states as a result of the disputed status of their borders contributes to these water tensions.

Regional Affairs

Regionally, Sino-Indian cooperation has been the exception rather than the rule. Beijing watches closely New Delhi's increasing engagement of East Asia, including relations with nations that have historically had particularly difficult interactions with Beijing, such as Japan, Vietnam, and Indonesia. At the same time, Indian strategists have expressed quiet concern over China's growing influence in the subcontinent, not only its maintenance of a robust political and military relationship with India's rival Pakistan, but also its extensive political, economic, and security relationship with Burma, growing relations with Bangladesh and Nepal, and increasing naval presence in the Indian Ocean. China's admission as an observer to the South Asian Association for Regional Cooperation (SAARC) in November 2005, with New Delhi's reluctant acquiescence, has been cited as further evidence of China's emergence as a player in India's backyard and the desire of India's smaller neighbours to draw China into the region as leverage.

India has viewed growing Chinese influence in Burma, which is strategically located along the eastern end of the Indian Ocean, with great suspicion. In the mid-1990s, India had been one of the most vocal and ardent supporters of Burma's democracy movement, led by Aung San Suu Kyi. However, the combination of India's aim to forge closer links with Southeast Asia as part of its "Look East" policy, its need for Burma's support in countering insurgent groups in India's northeast, its desire for access to Burma's natural resources, including energy (often in competition with China), and its alarm over China's growing military ties to the Burmese junta led India to adopt a more conciliatory engagement policy with the Burmese leadership by the late 1990s to counterbalance Chinese influence. Most notably, the presence of Chinese radar technicians in Burma's Coco Islands, which border India's Andaman and Nicobar

Islands, has fueled concern in New Delhi (and Washington) that Beijing is monitoring naval activities in the region.

Furthermore, China's efforts to develop alternative overland routes to transport oil and gas imports through port facilities at Gwadar in Pakistan's Baluchistan province, which is at the entrance of the Strait of Hormuz, as well as through Bangladesh and Burma, have been viewed by India as part of a Chinese "string of pearls" strategy of economic and military encroachment into South and Central Asia. Indeed, China's senior-most leaders have openly declared Beijing's attention to placing priority focus on naval modernization, including greater power-projection capability. Indian policymakers fear that China's moves could undermine India's regional preeminence.

At the same time, India's joint naval exercises in the South China Sea—with Vietnam in 2000 and Singapore in 2005, joint patrols with Indonesia in the Andaman Sea beginning in 2002, and exercises off the Japanese coast with the U.S. and Japanese navies in April 2007, have sparked concerns in Beijing. The Indian Navy, the world's fifth-largest, has also set up a Far Eastern Naval Command (FENC) off Port Blair on the Andaman Islands to increase its presence in the Strait of Malacca and potentially monitor Chinese naval activities in the region. Such mutual suspicions could result in China-Indian naval rivalry in and around the Indian Ocean over time.

For their part, East Asian nations have increasingly looked to India as a potential partner in economic and regional security affairs, with some, such as Japan, apparently considering India as a potential element in a hedging strategy against China. South Asian countries have likewise begun to play the "China card" in order to counterbalance India's influence in their affairs or gain policy concessions from India and the West.

For instance, as relations have soured between New Delhi and Dhaka in recent years, China has become Bangladesh's largest supplier of military hardware and has replaced India as Bangladesh's overall largest trading partner. In Nepal, China defied international suspension of military aid and other support to King Gyanendra's regime after the monarch suspended democracy from February 2005 to April 2006, calling the situation Nepal's "internal affair." King Gyanendra reciprocated by shutting down the office of the Dalai Lama's representative in Nepal as well as the Tibetan Refugee Welfare Office.

In the end, China and India each recognize the inexorable reality of the other's increasing involvement in its neighborhood. In response, the two nations are quietly balancing the prospects for cooperation and competition in their relationship without letting any residual suspicions, tensions, or mistrust derail their mutual desire to test the possibilities of political rapprochement, economic engagement, and confidence-building in the years ahead.

People-to-People Contacts

People-to-people contacts between China and India have increased in recent years, albeit from a low base. Regular direct flights were established in 2002, when China's tourism authorities designated India as an "authorized destination." More than 5,000 Indian students are currently studying in Chinese universities. In India, enthusiasm for Chinese popular culture is growing, and Indians tend to respect, if not envy, China's economic and political rise, which they would like to have their own country mirror. India dubbed 2006 the "Year of Friendship with China," and China declared 2007 the "Year of China-India Friendship through Tourism."

Nonetheless, while official interaction is on the rise and public opinion polls suggest that a majority of citizens and businessmen in both states hold favorable views of each other overall, popular interaction remains relatively minimal, restricted by the language barrier, cultural differences, and other factors. Chinese and Indian observers alike will note that the Chinese have more natural affinity with countries in East and Southeast Asia, while Indians are more comfortable in dealing with English-speaking countries and other South Asian states.

Mutual mistrust persists, particularly within India's older generation, whose memories of the Sino-Indian border conflict lead it to view China with suspicion. India's media and educational system have also nurtured the notion that China "stabbed India in the back" in 1962 and is sitting on Indian land. India's visa policy, in fact, is very restrictive and suspicious of the entry of citizens from China (among other nations, including the United States), further constraining popular contact.

For their part, the Chinese have expressed difficulty in understanding India's cultural and interpersonal style and have tended to be snobbish in their view of India and its state of development relative to China. While Indians may be focusing increasingly on China, relatively little Chinese popular attention is directed toward India. Few Chinese students study in India, for instance. Even at the official level, a similar lack of symmetry in the level of attention paid by China and India toward each other appears to prevail.

THE CHINA-INDIA BORDER ISSUE IN 2013: POINT AND COUNTER-POINT

On 15 April around thirty Chinese soldiers crossed an unguarded section of the China-India border – the Line of Actual Control (LAC) – and set up camp, reportedly nineteen kilometres inside territory India claims. In itself this was not an unheard of incident; one Indian newspaper reported that in 2012 there were 'over four hundred incursions', ninety per cent of which occurred in the Ladakh region, where the latest incident took place. This time, though, the Chinese troops set up a camp in the disputed territory, the first time they had done so since 1986.

A flag meeting was held by military representatives of the Indian and Chinese armies but to no avail. At subsequent meetings and through diplomatic channels, and amid much pressure from the mass media and the public, India asked China to withdraw to previously-held positions. China, in turn, asked India to remove the "fortified positions" its troops had constructed along the LAC.

The issue created a good deal of debate in China, India and the rest of the world, where it was reported upon and studied so as to deduce China's motivations for the "transgression" and India's strength and diplomatic maturity in how it dealt with it.

It is in this spirit of debate that Future Directions International presents this Associate Paper. Two noted analysts present the perspectives of China and India respectively. Dr. Liu Zongyi is a visiting fellow at the Centre for Strategic and International Studies (CSIS) and a research fellow at the Shanghai Institutes for International Studies (SIIS). Acknowledging the complexity of the border issue, Dr. Liu emphasises the symbiotic relationship between the two countries and observes India stands to gain more by allying with China rather than with the United States of America, with which country it is developing fast-growing ties.

Dr. Jabin Jacob is the Assistant Director & Fellow, Institute of Chinese Studies, New Delhi. Whilst not denying the complexity of the border issue, Dr. Jacob points out that incursions of this type will become the new norm and confidence-building measures will need to acknowledge this fact. He also notes that China, while acknowledging India's rise, appears to be unable to cast off its misgivings in relation to the growing India-US relationship.

SECTORS OF SINO-INDIAN BORDER: WESTERN SECTOR, MIDDLE SECTOR AND EASTERN SECTOR

The Sino-Indian border is generally divided into three sectors namely: (i) the Western sector, (ii) the Middle sector, and (iii) the Eastern sector.

The Western Sector

This 2,152 km long sector of the Sino-Indian border separates Jammu and Kashmir State of India from the Sinkiang province of China.

The frontier between Sinkiang and Pakistan occupied Kashmir (PoK) is about 480 km long. The rest is boundary between Ladakh and Tibet.

The boundary in the western sector runs along the Muztagh Ata Range and the Aghil Mountain across the Karakoram Pass via Quara Tagh pass and along the main Kunlun Range to a point east of 80°E longitude and 40 km north of Hajit Langer.

It forms a physical boundary between Gilgit area and Sinkiang following the main Karakoram watershed separating the streams flowing into the Indus basin from those flowing into the Tarin basin.

Farther south-east the boundary runs along the watershed across Lanak La, Kone La and Kepsang La, then follows the Chemesang River across Pergyon Lake and the Kailash Range. Here the boundary constitutes the watershed between the Indus system in India and the Khotan system in China.

The western sector boundary is the outcome of the British policy towards the state of Jammu and Kashmir. These boundaries were defined by the treaties of 1665 and 1686 (known as Ladakh-Tibet agreements) and were confirmed by 1842 Dogra-Ladakh agreement among Kashmir, Tibet and China.

However, this boundary was never delimited precisely on maps and has led to several boundary disputes between China and India. The Chinese claim rests mainly on ethnic grounds, and on the assertion that the wastelands of the Aksai Chin in disputed territory were always linked more with Tibet and Sinkiang.

The Chinese claim that Aksai Chin is just an extension of Tibet with regard to language, religion and culture. But in Chinese documentation regarding the actual occupation of the area by Tibet in inconclusive.

The Indians, on the other hand, claim that the area has been historically administered by the state of Jammu and Kashmir since 1849, and that the Indo-Tibet Treaties of 1665, 1684 and 1842 confirmed the boundary between Tibet and Ladakh.

China claims the Aksai Chin district, the Changmo valley, Pangong Tso and the Sponggar Tso area of north-east Ladakh as well as a strip of about 5,000 sq km down the entire length of eastern Ladakh. China also claims a part of Huza-Gilgit area in North Kashmir (ceded to it in 1963 by Pakistan), although the whole territory has been effectively under the British sovereignty since 1895.

Since 1954, the Chinese have repeatedly violated the international border between India and China and penetrated deep into the Indian Territory in the western sector. China renewed aggression in 1959 and the Line of Actual Control (LoAC) become of series of positions occupied by the Chinese forces rather than a well defined border between the two countries.

In 1962, China waged a full scale war and its forces intruded far deeper into the Indian Territory. Currently the Chinese occupation line runs 16 to 240 km west of traditional line. China is in actual possession of about 54,000 sq km of the Indian Territory of which 37,555 sq km is in Ladakh area alone.

The Middle Sector

The middle sector boundary between China and India is 625 km long and runs along the watershed from Ladakh to Nepal. Two Indian states of Himachal Pradesh and Uttaranchal touch this border. The boundary of Himachal Pradesh follows the water parting between the Spiti and Para Chu rivers and continues along the watershed between the eastern and western tributaries of the Satluj.

The Uttaranchal boundary is demarcated by the watershed between the Satluj on one hand and the Kali, the Alaknanda, and the Bhagirathi on the other. This boundary crosses the Satluj near the Shipki La on the Himachal-Tibet border.

Thereafter, it runs along the watershed passes of Mana, Niti, Kungri-Bingri, Dharma and Lipu Ladakh. It finally joins trijunction of China, India and Nepal. This part of the border was approved by the Tibetan and the British governments under the 1890 and 1919 treaties. Although there are not much serious territorial problems between the two countries, the Chinese lay claim on nearly 2,000 sq km area in this sector.

The Eastern Sector

The 1,140 km long boundary between India and China runs from the eastern limit of Bhutan to a point near Talu-Pass at the trijunction of India, Tibet and Myanmar. This line is usually referred to as the Me Mahon Line after Henry Me Mahon, a British representative who signed the 1913-14 Shimla Convention. This line normally runs along the crest of the Himalayas between Bhutan and Myanmar.

India has stressed that the Me Mahon Line is the international boundary between Tibet and India as was agreed to between the governments of India, China and Tibet. On the other hand China considers the Me Mahon line as illegal and unacceptable, claiming that Tibet had no right to sign the 1913-14 convention held in Shimla which delineated the Me Mahon Line on the map.

India challenges such a position, maintaining that Tibet was independent and in fact concluded several independent treaties which were considered valid by all parties, and were in operation for decades.

China declined the validity of the Me Mahon Line as an international boundary and laid claims to areas south of this line up to the foot of the Himalayan range in the Brahmaputra valley. The whole of Arunachal Pradesh, measuring over 88 thousand sq km has been claimed by China as the Chinese territory. This area has been administered by India since 1947.

Chinese government never formally questioned the validity of 1913-14 Shimla convention until 1959. India has been striking at the two crucial points. First, Britain and India had been exercising jurisdiction over the area since 1914 and 1947 respectively and second China never disputed the Indian control over the area until 1959.

Even in 1956 when the Chinese attention was drawn to certain maps drawn by China which showed these areas to be parts of China, the Chinese government promised to look into the 'cartographic errors' in their maps.

China's relations with India started taking a bad turn in 1950s when China started consolidating its position in Tibet and then in Ladakh. By 1956, China started intensifying its intrusions into the Indian Territory. India wishfully hoped that the insurmountable barrier of the Himalayas would prevent Chinese to attack Indian Territory. Indian apprehensions grew in 1956 when China built a road through Ladakh linking West Tibet with Sinkiang and quickly moved into Aksai Chin and eastern Ladakh. China also moved its forces into the North-East Frontier Agency (NEFA), the present Arunachal Pradesh.

Reported small-scale armed clashes between 1959 and 1962 escalated into a full-scale war in October, 1962 when China launched a major offensive in Ladakh in the western sector and NEFA in the eastern sector. Indian armed forces were not well trained to fight a modern war in a rough and rugged mountainous terrain. They were outnumbered and outgunned by the Chinese forces.

Following lessons have been learnt from Chinese aggression over India:

(i) The myth that the Himalayas were an effective defense barrier was exploded.

(ii) India's naive confidence in China's friendliness had dulled its perception regarding effective security measures in the Indo-China borderlands.

(iii) The prompt and positive response of western countries in rushing military supplies to the war zone helped improve the image of the West in Indian eyes.

(iv) India realised that posture of "non-alignment" was no substitute for defense preparedness.

Surprisingly, Chinese forces pulled back without annexing the disputed territory in the eastern sector. In the western sector, however, they did not pull out of most of Aksai Chin. Perhaps they did so due to the fear that their advance troops would have been cut off from supply bases in Tibet in winter of 1962 when the high passes in the Himalayas would have been closed by snow. The Chinese justified their withdrawal by stating that they had no further territorial ambitions. The primary aim of Chinese invasion was to deprive India of its moral leadership in the world especially among the Afro-Asian countries, and to put pressure on it to join the socialist camp. China's collusion with Pakistan is a clear indication of this political ambition.

Perhaps China miscalculated its political power strategy. The support of the Western countries to India compelled China to rethink its strategy. India's unity in the face of Chinese aggression was another deterrent for China to achieve political mileage.

An uneasy truce had been prevailing for a long time since the October, 1962 war. Neither side made a serious effort to normalise the situation on the border. The Colombo powers, spearheaded by Ceylon (now Sri Lanka) and the erstwhile Soviet Union failed to bring about a respectable agreement between the two countries. Several countries condemned China as an aggressor. However, Cuba, Albania and Portugal supported the Chinese.

Of late, leaders of both the countries have engaged themselves in improving the bilateral relations. Several meetings have been held to resolve the problem of border issues. A major development took place in October, 2003 when China made a significant change in its official website. It removed the mention of Sikkim from its list of nations.

In May, 2004, China recognised Sikkim as a part of India for the first time. The world map in World Affairs Year Book 2003/2004 does not show Sikkim as separate country in Asia. It also does not mention Sikkim in its index of countries.

The move was significant since it involves recognition of Sikkim-China border which is a part of the Me Mahon Line. If things go as planned, the two nations should be able to work out the guide lines for transforming the Line of Actual Control (LoAC) into a mutually acceptable and internationally recognised boundary. However, China still insists that Arunachal Pradesh is a disputed territory.

China has also suggested a 'package deal'. It asked India to accept Chinese domination over Aksai Chin in return of China's acceptance of Me Mahon Line as the international boundary. India, however, has advocated 'sector-by-sector' approach. Indian side is hopeful because China has settled border disputes with Russia and Vietnam.

SINO-INDIAN BORDER DISPUTE AND THE ROLE OF TIBET

The era of the late 19th century and the early 20th century was ripe with the European colonial powers finding new ways of exerting their influence in Asia and dividing it up.

Tibet was no exception. For years, many kings and empires, from Muhammad Tukluq to the British, had tried to wrench Tibet from China, with no significant successes.

Finally, the British came up with an underhand ploy to divide Tibet from within; so as to create a buffer state between British India and China; just as Mongolia had been divided and part of it made into a buffer between Russia and China. Sir Henry McMahon proposed the division of Tibet into an 'inner' and 'outer' Tibet. The Chinese representative saw through British imperial designs and smelt a rat; and thus left the Simla conference.

But the matter didn't end there. A note was appended to the Simla accord, thatcontained a map showing a part of Tibetan (i.e. Chinese) territory as Indian, based on a thick red line known as the McMahon line. Furthermore, China was barred from any rights and privileges of the Accord with respect to Tibet.

DISPUTED TERRITORIES

The major territories disputed between these two countries can be divided into two distinct parts:

1) The Western Sector - Aksai Chin, which lies to the east of the Kashmir valley, covering an area of about 37,250 sq.km (14,380 sq.mi) - currently occupied by China.

2) The Eastern Sector - Most of the Indian state of Arunachal Pradesh, that China calls South Tibet, covering an area of 83,743 sq.km (32,333 sq.mi) - currently occupied by India.

In addition to these, there are also a few small chunks of territory in between these two sectors, but they are largely irrelevant when compared to these two major distinct territories.

THE MCMAHON LINE

The McMahon line is the basis of the Indian claim to the area that was formerly known as the North-East Frontier Agency; and has since become the Indian state of Arunachal Pradesh. It was drawn with a complete disregard for cartographic techniques and the geography of the area. The scale was - eight miles to an inch.

AKSAI CHIN

Historical claims on the Aksai China area are even more dubious. There has never been any concrete demarcation of this region.

Britain was concerned about Russia's designs in this area, and hence proposed to make the Karakorum Pass as the boundary, so as to again create a buffer between Xinjiang/ China and India.

As author Neville Maxwell states,

"In early 1880s, China and India agreed the Karakoram Pass as the fixed point of boundary, while leaving both sides of the pass indefinite. In the mid-1890s, China claimed Aksai Chin as its territory, and voiced the claim to Macartney in 1896, who drew part of the British boundary in the Himalayas. Macartney presented the claim to the British who agreed with his comment that part of Aksai Chin was in China and part in the British territory. Meanwhile, the forward school of British strategist in London suggested that the British should not only include the whole of Aksai Chin, but also all the territory given to Kashmir in 1865."

In 1899, the British proposed to China that the whole of Aksai Chin would remain Chinese territory and the boundary would be along the Karakorum range; which is the status quo today. The Karakorum pass falls precisely on the boundary of territory controlled by India and China, marking northern end of Sino-Indian border, known as the Line of Actual Control.

However, China didn't reply to this proposal, something which it would regret for years. If it had, the fate of Aksai Chin would have been sealed then and there.

Nehru, for his part, appeared willing to play down the Indian claims to the Aksai Chin. He tried to delay disclosure if the news that the Chinese had built a road in the area. After the news had been revealed, he sought to play down the economic significance of the area, describing it as "barren tundra" and where "not even a blade of grass grows". He even went so far as to cast doubt on the validity of the Indian claim to Aksai Chin.

In statements to the Indian Parliament during early 1959, Nehru pointed out that

"...during British rule, this area was neither inhabited: nor were there any outposts,........this place, Aksai Chin area, is distinguished completely from other areas. It is a matter for argument which part belongs to us and which part belongs to somebody else. It is not clear".

Britain's Flip-Flops

Around that time, it was understood by the British government that Tibet forms part of Chinese territory. According to the Anglo-Russian Convention of 1907, both players of the so called 'Great Game', Britain and Russia, had decided to negotiate with Tibet only through China. According to the Anglo-Chinese Convention of 1906, Britain was "not to annex Tibetan territory". British Journalist Neville Maxwell states that McMahon had been instructed not to sign bilaterally with the Tibetans if China refused.

But that was exactly what McMahon did, previous promises be damned. Britain and Tibet signed the agreement themselves without Chinese knowledge, and was thus rejected at first by the British government in London. (Later however, its stance seems to have changed; and then changed again, as discussed below). Tibet welcomed this treaty because it would give further credence to what it thought was its 'sovereignty', even if it came at the cost of territory. Accordingly, the purpose and content of these exchanges had to be kept secret, and not only from the Chinese.

Britain seems to have taken upon itself the role of Tibet's Guardian. In the 1940s, British officials in India pointed out to Anthony Eden, the then British Foreign Secretary, that China had no rights in Tibet since it had not accepted the provisions of the Simla accord of 1914 (As if it was up to Britain to decide the extent of China's 'right' to Tibet!). Needless to say, the Tibetan government welcomed these intrusions.

Initially, London rejected the Simla accord as it was in contradiction with many previous agreements. But later, in 1935, some hardliners within the government convinced it to start using the line on official maps - thus officially accepting that the McMahon line was the official border between India and Tibet (and hence, later China too).

But recently in 2008, a historic statement was released by the British Foreign Office which would have far reaching consequences. The British government discarded the Simla agreement as an anachronism and a colonial legacy - a "position [the British] took based on the geo-politics of the time". The British pulled away the only leg India had to stand on.

The statement says,

".......our position is unusual for one reason of history that has been imported into the present: the anachronism of our formal position on whether Tibet is part of China, and whether in fact we harbour continued designs to see the break up of China. We do not."

"Our ability to get our points across has sometimes been clouded by the position the UK took at the start of the 20th century on the status of Tibet, a position based on the geo-

politics of the time. Our recognition of China's "special position" in Tibet developed from the outdated concept of suzerainty. "

(A New York Times article about this statement, entitled, 'Did Britain just sell Tibet?' (as if Britain owned it!) accused the British of 'rewriting history' in exchange for China's support during the financial crisis!)

Effectively, what Britain in fact was saying was that Tibet is a part of China and is not sovereign - which was the position of almost all countries by that time, including EU nations and the US. It even apologized for not having done so earlier. However, what is important in that statement is that the British seem to have completely discarded the Simla agreement - on which the whole of India's negotiating stance is based. Consequently, if we start with the assumption that the Simla agreement was illegal as Tibet had no right to conclude treaties separately, then we arrive at what the Chinese position has been all along!

THE TIBETAN QUESTION AND THE CAUSE OF THE DISPUTE

The fact is that a large part of the border dispute hinges on the uncomfortable question of Tibet's sovereignty. If Tibet was sovereign at the time of the Simla conference, then the treaty is legal and it serves India's cause. If Tibet was not sovereign at that time, then the treaty is illegal and serves China's cause.

Some activists campaigning for a free Tibet often bring up the Simla conference as proof of Tibet's independence. Their arguments are mainly two fold -

a) The Tibetan representative signed the treaty even though he was instructed by the Chinese representative not to sign, a clear indication undermining (Tibetan acceptance of) Chinese suzerainty over Tibet.

b) More importantly, since Tibet concluded a treaty with a foreign power on its own,*it was an independent country on that day.*

At the time of the Simla conference, although the Tibetan government had driven out all Chinese officials from Tibet after the collapse of the Qing dynasty and declared independence, the Nationalist government did not accept this and neither has the PRC nor any other government.

India had enjoyed certain privileges with regard to Tibet under the Simla Agreement, including those regarding trade and commerce. However, when China 'annexed' Tibet in 1951, India under Nehru recognized it as Chinese territory, thus giving up those privileges and undermining Tibet's sovereignty (which it may have momentarily enjoyed during the time of the Simla agreement). Thus in a sense the Indian government tacitly admitted that the Simla agreement was effectively illegal, which to this day remains China's official position. In doing so, India weakened its own position with respect to the border dispute. The Simla agreement was signed between Britain, Tibet and China. Now, from this information, two questions present themselves -

1) If Tibet *was* sovereign, why was China invited at the conference at all? Why didn't the British negotiate directly with Tibet?
2) If Tibet was *not* sovereign, why was *it* invited at the conference? Why didn't the British negotiate directly with China? (In other words, why did China accept to attend a conference where Tibet was represented as a separate party?)

The answer to (1) is that, as stated above, Britain recognised Tibet to be under Chinese suzerainty. Hence, any *bilateral* agreement that Britain signed with Tibet (without Chinese agreement) would be illegal. (But ironically, that is exactly what the British did)

(2) is a bit more complicated. There are indications that the British had blackmailed the Chinese into attending by threatening to -

a) withdraw their recognition of the new nationalist government, and,

b) sign the treaty with Tibet alone if China didn't participate, thus acknowledging that Tibet was in fact sovereign. (But later the British did exactly the same thing when China didn't agree to its terms during the conference).

Hence, it is clear that Britain's imperial designs and its policy of 'divide and rule' and double crossing everyone was in effect the cause of the entire dispute.

INDIA'S RELATIONS WITH CHINA: THE GOOD, THE BAD AND THE (POTENTIALLY) UGLY

Later this month, Indian Prime Minister Manmohan Singh will travel to Beijing. The visit will cap a year that has been full of ups and downs in India's relations with China. The tale of three trips is representative. One in May by Chinese Premier Li Keqiang, his first abroad, was intended to signal the importance Beijing placed in the Sino-Indian relationship. But it took place in the aftermath of—and some would say was overshadowed by—a border standoff between the two countries' militaries. In July, the Indian defense minister visited Beijing to rebuild trust and defense ties. Media coverage, however, focused on warnings to India issued by a PLA general, which Chinese officials had to rush to dismiss.

And Singh will be travelling from a country that is largely preoccupied domestically. When discussions do turn to China, they have focused on concerns about Indian capacity vis-à-vis that country, Indian politicians accusing the government of being soft on China and Chinese scholars labeling India's border infrastructure upgrades as provocative. These and other developments have highlighted what Indian policymakers acknowledge—that there are elements of cooperation, competition and concern in the China-India relationship.

There have been good signs for those interested in stable, cooperative Sino-Indian relations.In the spring, just after he'd formally taken office, Chinese President Xi Jinping proposed a five-point formula to improve ties between the two countries.

"Positive vibes" were detected at Xi's subsequent meeting with Singh on the sidelines of the BRICS summit in Durban in March. There have been numerous public Chinese declarations of the importance of the relationship—perhaps not seen since the first half of the 1950s. The Chinese ambassador to India unusually took to the editorial pages of an Indian newspaper to emphasize, "To strengthen good-neighbourly and friendly cooperation with India is China's strategic choice and established policy which will not change." Chinese officials have indicated that greater efforts should be made toward a boundary settlement. The two countries have strategic and economic dialogues in place. They restarted their defense dialogue earlier this year and are expected to resume joint military exercises shortly. China and India also have specialized dialogues on issues like Afghanistan, Central Asia and counterterrorism. The agreement to discuss Afghanistan was considered a departure from previous Chinese policy; Beijing had earlier been reluctant to add it to the agenda because it would have likely meant talking about Chinese ally Pakistan. Along with regional discussions, China and India have also cooperated in the multilateral realm, including on issues like trade and climate change.

Premier Li chose India as his first overseas stop, with the Chinese government indicating that the choice was very deliberate. Hosting an Indian youth delegation, Li put a personal spin on the choice, noting the "the seeds of friendship sown" when he visited India 27 years ago—a trip that he said left a "lasting impact." During the May visit, he stressed the need to build trust and especially emphasized the economic benefits of greater ties.

Those economic ties have already grown. China is one of India's largest trading partners. Bilateral trade in goods has gone from less than $3 billion in 2000 to $66.57 billion in 2012. While investments haven't kept the same pace, they have also grown. In India, the interest in doing business with China is evident beyond the private sector and the central government—along with visits by a number of Indian CEOs, China has also seen visits from chief ministers of a number of Indians states, including Andhra Pradesh, Bihar, Karnataka and Madhya Pradesh. Narendra Modi, current chief minister of the state of Gujarat and prime ministerial candidate for the forthcoming national election for the BJP (India's largest opposition party), has also traveled to China. While Modi has expressed hawkish views on China on the geopolitical front, he has expressed admiration for that country's economic achievements.

The governments of both countries have reasons for wanting stable ties: the desire for a peaceful periphery in order to focus on domestic socio-economic objectives; the need for stability in South Asia, especially with the impending American drawdown of forces from Afghanistan; existing and potential economic ties; and the prospect for cooperation in the multilateral realm. For Delhi, in addition, a stable relationship with China opens up the possibility that Beijing might use its leverage with Islamabad to shape Pakistan's behavior in a way that might benefit India. For Beijing, there's desire to limit India's burgeoning relationships with the United States and Japan, as well as with other countries in what Beijing considers its backyard. Moreover, as China is preoccupied with eastern maritime disputes and the North Korean situation, stable relations on its southern and southwestern flank would also help the Chinese leadership.

This year has, however, also shown how quickly the bad in the relationship can steal the spotlight from the good—with the potential to turn ugly. In April, less than two weeks after an Indian observer commented on the "upswing in relations" between China and India, their long-standing boundary dispute flared once again. While the two countries communicated through the crisis and resolved it diplomatically, and Li's visit proceeded as planned, the border incident reinforced the mistrust that many in India feel toward China and its intentions. Furthermore, it was a reminder that despite increased engagement, bilateral differences have the potential to stall, if not reverse, progress toward more stable relations.

Differences are not restricted to the boundary dispute. Tibet remains a key source of tension between the two countries though the two countries have found a way to manage their differences on the issue for now. In addition, China's relationship with Pakistan has been a major source of concern in India. Its role in strengthening Pakistan's conventional, missile and nuclear capabilities is especially highlighted. India also disapproves of China's assistance to Pakistan in developing projects and infrastructure in area disputed between India and Pakistan.

China's growing political and economic ties with India's neighbors are also a subject of concern. Delhi watches warily increasing Chinese interactions—political and commercial—with and involvement in countries like Afghanistan, Bangladesh, Myanmar, Nepal and Sri Lanka. Concern about a military dimension being added persists. Beijing's increasing interest in operating in the Indian Ocean, which India has traditionally considered its backyard, has also not gone unnoticed. While China emphasizes that these activities have benign goals—economic development, security for its ships, etc.—some in India who tend to take a hawkish position are not convinced; others are taking a wait-and-see attitude. Even beyond the neighborhood, there are concerns about competition with China for markets, influence and resources across the globe.

Closer to home, water is the resource that has become the subject of tension—specifically Chinese dam construction on its side of the Brahmaputra River. Indian officials have publiclycalled for Beijing to reassure India on this matter. Domestic critics, however, perceive the Indian government as being too tolerant of the construction. They argue that China has not respected information sharing agreements on this front and warn of more ambitiousChinese river diversion plans.

Economic ties, which many envisioned as the driver of good Sino-Indian ties, have also not escaped trouble. Bilateral trade in goods actually fell almost 10 percent from 2011 to 2012. In India there's much concern about the trade imbalance. The overall trade deficit has gonefrom $28 billion in 2010-2011 to

$40.8 billion in 2012-2013. While investments have grown, they remain limited compared to the investment relationships that both China and India have with other countries. In India, there have also been complaints about market access in China and the treatment of Indian labor there, concern about Chinese investment in "strategic" sectors in India, accusations about visa abuses by Chinese companies and restrictions on Chinese labor. Indian companies also privately express concerns about cyber-espionage. Overall, reports of cyber-attacks on Indian government and military networks—allegedly emanating from China—have done nothing to decrease distrust that persists, especially among the public.

There is also an overall sense that China does not respect India and/or that it will seek to prevent India's rise. As evidence, critics point not only to China's relationship with Pakistan, which is seen as driven by a desire to keep India tied up in South Asia, but also note China'sreluctance to endorse India's demand for a permanent seat on the U.N. Security Council or its objections to India being given membership in the Nuclear Suppliers Group.

Another overarching problem: the lack of trust in China and its intentions. This is especially evident among the public. According to a Pew poll last year, more Indians have an unfavorable view of China than a favorable view. In a more recent Lowy Institute poll, China ranked only second to Pakistan in terms of countries that people considered threatening to India, with 60 percent indicating China would be a major threat over the next decade (an additional 22 percent identified it as a minor threat). 73 percent of those surveyed identified "war with China" as a big threat over the next ten years. Almost three-quarters believed that China wants to dominate Asia. 58 percent felt that China's growth had not been good for India. This reinforces what the Pew poll found last year. In that poll, two-thirds of urbanites who expressed an opinion on the subject believed that China's growing economy was a bad thing.

Overcoming this mistrust continues to be a major obstacle. The legacy of history remains a problem. Every time there is a border incident it reinforces the narrative that has prevailed in many quarters in India since the 1962 China-India war: that China only understands strength; that while Beijing's leaders say China and India "must shake hands," they cannot be trusted—that one hand held out might just be a precursor to the other stabbing one in the back. This problem is made worse by limited connectivity and communications, and little knowledge about the other country—even though these have improved. Media coverage about China and the relationship can also get quite heated, with a tendency to focus on the negative. All these problems are exacerbated by the lack of transparency when it comes to Chinese decision-making. This has led to uncertainty about Chinese behavior and motivations, which was evident in the debate about why the border incident in April occurred—and this uncertainty exists even among policymakers.

Thus, Indian governments have tried to follow a multi-pronged strategy. The emphasis might have differed somewhat, but for the last two governments in India—one a coalition led by the BJP and the current one led by the Congress—the general approach towards China has been to co-operate, if possible, and to compete, if necessary. Indian officials have joined with Chinese counterparts to increase ties, build trust and improve communications. Simultaneously, policymakers note that competition in and of itself is not all bad. As former Indian Prime Minister Vajpayee noted in Beijing, "a sense of competition between two close and equal neighbours" might indeed be natural. There is also, however, a realization that beyond cooperation and competition, there is a potential for conflict. Thus, while hoping and working for the best, there has been some attention on planning and preparing for the worst—i.e. the possibility that China will emerge as an explicit threat. There is a desire to do this cautiously, however, with policymakers quite conscious of the potential for provocation, miscalculation and exacerbation of the security dilemma.

In practice, this overall approach has meant increasing engagement with China—political, economic and even military-to-military—at the bilateral, regional and multilateral levels. Simultaneously, this approach has translated to a series of actions including strengthening India's military, as well as its border infrastructure and border regions, maintaining a nuclear deterrent, and consolidating or expanding ties and influence in India's near abroad.

India has also tried to step up its game in China's neighborhood. Indian policymakers underplay the strategic aspects and goals of India's "Look East" policy—which the Indian foreign ministry describes as "oriented towards deepening India's engagement with the countries of East and Southeast Asia"—and emphasize its cultural and economic aspects. However, these elements and the link to China have not been entirely missing in action. The Indian government and companies are increasingly interested and engaged in the region, especially focusing on countries like Indonesia, Japan, Singapore, Thailand and Vietnam. In recent months, India-Japan ties have probably been in the spotlight the most, with another round of the U.S.-India-Japan trilateral dialogue and Singh's visit to Japan in May. India has also sought to be more engaged with multilateral fora in the region. Officials from some Southeast Asian countries, however, want India to do much more. Channeling some of their frustrations, Hillary Clinton, when she led the State Department, called for "India not just to look east, but to engage East and act East as well."

Another key aspect of India's approach has been the pursuit of closer relations with the United States. Of course, these ties with the United States are not solely driven by China. India indeed has no desire to make a choice between its relations with China and the United States. However, the United States plays a useful role as an offshore balancer. Furthermore, Indian policymakers believe that a strong U.S.-India relationship gives them leverage with China and sends a signal to that country. Some also note that China takes India more seriously because the United States does. India, however, still has doubts about U.S. reliability as a potential partner, especially given the level of Sino-U.S. engagement, and prefers to maintain a diversified portfolio of partnerships. So, where do India's relations with China go from here? In the near term, during the Prime Minister's visit, the two sides might sign a border defense cooperation agreement. The accord would essentially be a way to manage rather than resolve the boundary question, which the Indian foreign secretary has noted continues to be "a particularly difficult issue." The trans-border rivers question is also likely to be discussed. In addition, given the two countries' priorities, bilateral and global economic and financial issues will be high on the agenda. Potentially, there also might be agreements that could facilitate greater people-to-people ties, including a cultural and visa pacts. Regionally, developments vis-à-vis Afghanistan and the Middle East that concern both governments are likely to be discussed. Finally, on the multilateral front, trade and climate change issues might be on the agenda, given upcoming international summits in those two areas.

As for the longer term, the scenarios usually outlined are deepening cooperation, increasing competition that might lead to conflict, or continuity with both competition and cooperation in evidence. There is a debate in India—inside and outside government—about China, which scenario might prevail, the future of the relationship and what approach to take with China. The differences are evident in the Lowy poll—almost equal numbers of those surveyed believe that India "should join with other countries to limit China's influence" and "should cooperate with China to play a leading role in the world together."

How the relationship plays out will depend on a number of internal, bilateral, regional and global factors. In the meantime, Shyam Saran, a former foreign secretary and currently chairman of the National Security Advisory Board, has called for India to manage relations with China "with prudence but firmness." An air force chief described the way forward as "play cool and continue to develop capabilities."

5

China-India Border Tension : Doklam Plateau Buildup

Prime Minister Narendra Modi and external affairs minister Sushma Swaraj of misleading the nation over Chinese troops occupying the Doklam plateau, saying Indian security and strategic interests have been compromised. "The satellite imagery and media reports suggest that China has established military establishments in Doklam near Indian borders which indicates that India's security and strategic interests have been compromised," said Congress spokesperson Randeep Singh Surjewala.

The Congress' reaction comes a day after media reports cited new satellite images to say that the infrastructure build-up in Doklam — the site of a tense standoff between the two countries last summer — included a "full-fledged" military base. ThePrint described one of the constructions as "concrete" and said that there was at least one complete mechanised regiment deployed. According to NDTV, the build-up was at two locations at the Doklam plateau and one of them was "a massive, full-fledged Chinese military complex".

"It seems that the government was snoozing while the Chinese troops occupied the Doklam plateau as suggested by satellite images. And it seems China is planning Doklam 2.0 like retreat near the Indian borders," said Surjewala. "The Prime Minister has mastered the art of electoral rhetoric as he has failed miserably to ensure the protection of our borders."

Showing the satellite images, Surjewala said China had constructed a two-storey watch tower, seven helipads and several military establishments in Doklam.

"What is the government doing as China has occupied the entire Doklam plateau? Is the government, Prime Minister, defence minister aware of these constructions?" Slamming Swaraj, Surjewala said the ministry of external affairs had issued a statement after the end of the three-month Doklam standoff, saying the troops of both countries were doing expeditious disengagement.

"Even Sushma Swarajji said (this) in Parliament. And when we asked about the details, she said the troops of both countries were returning to their posts. At that point, there was no reason to question her statement," he said.

He said after the tensions at Doklam were resolved, the Chinese foreign ministry had said while it had withdrawn the troops, it shall keep on patrolling the area.

The Congress leader demanded to know how the issue of tri-junction at Doklam would be decided in future when the China had occupied the entire plateau. Surjewala said: "In October, Modiji announced at a public rally that Doklam issue as a victory. However, the satellite imagery released in media reports suggest that Chinese troops have constructed military establishments. On Wednesday, Indian army chief General Bipin Rawat said the Chinese military has carried out a "mostly temporary" buildup in Doklam. "They have carried out some infrastructure development, most of it is temporary in nature. But while their troops may have returned and the infrastructure remains, it is anybody's guess whether they would come back there, or it is because of the winter they could not take their equipment away," Rawat said during a session in the multi-lateral 'Raisina Dialogue'.

DEVELOPMENT ON THE DOKLAM PLATEAU

Since the tense June 2017 standoff between China and India on the Doklam or Donglang plateau, China has taken significant steps to improve its defensive posture and military infrastructure in the region. These developments emerged at a significant pace.

The Doklam plateau is a disputed area between China and Bhutan, India supports the Bhutanese claim, but China currently controls the area. The area is strategically important to India and China as it leads to the Indian Siliguri corridor, often referred to the chicken's neck, which connects India's northeastern states to the rest of the country.

In June, Chinese road construction in the area prompted an Indian response on the behalf of Bhutan, attempting to halt the construction. The altercation resulted in a standoff and scuffles between Indian and Chinese troops. After online sources spent most January and February pointing out Chinese buildup in and around Doklam, the Indian Ministry of Defense gave a statement on March 7 that China and India "redeployed" after the summer 2017 disengagement.

Chinese developments on the plateau include a dense network of trenches densely covering areas surrounding the strategic road leading to India. Additionally, China has built helipads, storage sites for vehicles, and new roads, as well as widened existing roads to allow for greater logistical capabilities in the event of open conflict.

In the satellite image above, light turquoise lines mark new trench lines, while red lines mark new roads and old roads now widened or otherwise improved. White diamonds mark newly constructed vehicle depots and military installations. White circles mark newly constructed helipads. The entire area measures about 3.5 miles (5.6 km) across, and 2.5 miles (4 km) in depth.

The below provides imagery from just prior to the standoff, compared to imagery of recent Chinese development in the region. The slider also depicts some of the improved Indian infrastructure in the area directly adjacent to the Indian border. This includes, but is not limited to, a new paved road leading directly up to the Chinese Donglang border road.

Chinese developments use established roads under their control as a base for branching out with smaller roads and trench systems. This expansion occurred primarily in the western direction towards India, but also southward on strategically important hilltops, deeper into Bhutan. The mountainsides on the de jure Sino-Bhutanese border are covered in the most expansive and systematic trench systems in the area, whereas trench systems closer to the de facto Sino-Indian border are more organic.

The above satellite imagery originated from December 9, 2017, at which point most construction had reached its conclusion. Here, three helicopter landing pads have been added in a newly-constructed area for storing military materiel. A protective berm covered the backside of camouflage nets on the storage site in which the northernmost helipad resided.

The second graphic presented a much larger storage area, slightly further down the road, closer to the de facto Sino-Indian border. The site was still under construction in the imagery and trails left behind form temporary camps suggested that troops stationed in the area have moved to more permanent basing.

The third graphic, which was the closest of the samples to the Indian border, depicted an entrenched area for storage as well as a surrounding trench system. The presence of trench systems had nothing to do with their proximity to India, as more expansive trench systems exist further back.

Finally, the newly widened main road leading from China into Doklam is now radically different, and can accommodate better for more, heavier traffic. The road has also been lined with trench systems and various other infrastructure.

Naturally, the strengthening of forward positions did not occur in strategic isolation, but in the context of a bolstered military infrastructure in depth. According to open source research, China has been improving its capacity to accommodate a greater numbers of troops, materiel, and air power to rapidly deploy to the region.

Conclusions

After the summer 2017 standoff in Doklam, China has taken measures to ensure its supremacy in the plateau. These measures include traditional defensive measures such as expansive trench systems and logistical improvements to accommodate for, and sustain, a sudden surge in troop presence. These developments have not only improved the Chinese defensive posture in the area, but also its offensive. China has not been unilateral in developing its military infrastructure in the area, India has maintained trench systems on the de facto border long before, and has constructed a new road leading up to the plateau in the past year.

CHINA BUILDING UP MILITARY CAPABILITY NEAR DOKLAM

While suggesting that India treat its bilateral relations with it from long-term perspective with a global vision and asking it not to be bogged down by some specific bilateral issues, China has been busy building up its military forces near the Doklam plateau, the site of a protracted June-Aug stand-off between the two sides, according to Indian media reports Dec 14, citing satellite pictures. Analysts have been cited as suggesting the development would allow China to tighten its control of its borders and prepare for any future problems in the region. In this connection, China is said to be also improving its military infrastructure, including with new mortar and gun positions, at a site between five and 10km from the site of this summer's 73-day stand-off, with Indian media reports citing satellite imagery acquired on Dec 3.

The images are also said to show the presence of at least nine three-storey buildings and almost 300 large vehicles, suggesting the stationing of almost a whole troop division in Yadong County in Tibet. China is also stated to have deployed troops 50km further away in the Chumbi Valley, where the borders of India, China and Bhutan meet, reported the Indian news portal *ThePrint*.

On Dec 10, *The Times of India* reported that China had permanently stationed up to 1,800 troops in Doklam, near the Sikkim-Bhutan-Tibet tri-junction, apparently to stay there for the whole of the winter. It also said China had built two helipads and installed scores of pre-fabricated huts, shelters and stores there, adding that existing roads had been relaid.

The troops may have stepped back after the summer standoff, but the China-India dispute in the Himalayas is obviously far from over. Although the build-up has not spilt over to other territories, another stand-off in Doklam could not be ruled out, the *scmp.com* Dec 14 cited observers as saying.

The Doklam standoff had ended when Indian troops retreated and China stopped the road building that had triggered the dispute. But China was obviously not at all happy with the settlement and its official media only reported about India having withdrawn from the site while suggesting it was still maintaining its presence at Doklam.

Meanwhile, Lt Gen Abhay Krishna, India's General Officer Commanding-in-Chief of the Eastern Command has on Dec 16 said India was totally geared up to face any situation in the Doklam sector. While refusing to name anyone specifically, he has said the Indian Army was in high spirits and ready to take on any mischief. "We are totally prepared, geared up; let anybody do any mischief and he will get it back nice and proper," India's *PTI* news agency quoted him as saying.

SINO-BHUTANESE BORDER DISPUTE AT DOKLAM

Authoritative depictions of historical Chinese maps by the People's Republic of China show Sikkim and Bhutan as part of Tibet or China for a period of 1800 years, starting from the second century B.C. From 1958, Chinese maps started showing large parts of Bhutanese territory as part of China. In 1960, China issued a statement claiming that Bhutan, Sikkim and Ladakh were part of a unified family in Tibet and had always been subject to the "great motherland of China". Alarmed,

Bhutan closed off its border with China and shut all trade and diplomatic contacts. It also established formal defense arrangements with India.

1960s

Starting August 1965, China and India traded accusations regarding intrusions into Doklam. China alleged that Indian troops were crossing into Doklam (which they called "Dognan") from Doka La, and were carrying out reconnaissance and intimidating Chinese herders. At first, the Indians paid no attention to the complaint. However, after several rounds of exchanges, on 30 September 1966, they forwarded a protest from the Bhutanese government which stated that Tibetan grazers were entering the pastures near the Doklam plateau accompanied by Chinese patrols. The letter asserted that the Doklam area was to the "south of the traditional boundary between Bhutan and the Tibet region" in the southern Chumbi area. On 3 October, the Government of Bhutan issued a press statement in which it said, "this area is traditionally part of Bhutan and no assertion has been made by the Government of the People's Republic of China disputing the traditional frontier which runs along recognizable natural features."

In response, the Chinese government replied that Bhutan was a sovereign country and that China did not recognize any role for the Indian government in the matter. It also asserted that the Doklam area had "always been under Chinese jurisdiction", that the Chinese herdsmen had "grazed cattle there for generations" and that the Bhutanese herdsmen had to pay pasturage to the Chinese side to graze cattle there. China later formally extended claims to 300 sq. miles of territory in northern Bhutan and areas north of Punakha, but apparently not in Doklam. Bhutan requested the Indian government to raise the matter with China. However, China rejected India's initiatives stating that the issue concerned China and Bhutan alone. Indian commentators state that the Chinese troops withdrew after a month and that the fracas over Doklam brought Bhutan even closer to India, resulting in the appointment of

3,400 Indian defence personnel in Bhutan for training the Bhutanese Army.

Border negotiations

Border negotiations between Bhutan and China began in 1972 with India playing a supporting role. However, China sought the exclusion of India. Bhutan commenced its own border negotiations with China in 1984. Prior to putting forward its claim line, it carried out its own surveys and produced maps that were approved by the National Assembly in 1989. Strategic expert Manoj Joshi states that the Bhutanese voluntarily shed territory in the process. Other scholars noted a reduction of 8,606 km area in the official Bhutanese maps. The Kula Kangri mountain, touted as the tallest peak in Bhutan, has apparently been ceded to China.

Bhutan said that, through the course of border talks, it had reduced 1,128 km of disputed border areas to 269 km by 1999. In 1996, the Chinese negotiators offered a "package deal" to Bhutan, offering to give up claims on 495 km^2 in the central region in exchange for 269 km^2 in the "northwest", i.e., adjacent to the Chumbi valley, including Doklam, Sinchulumpa, Dramana and Shakhatoe. These areas would offer strategic depth to Chinese defences and access to the strategic Siliguri Corridor of India. Bhutan turned down the offer, allegedly under Indian persuasion.

Having turned down China's package deal, in 2000, Bhutanese government put forward its original claim line of 1989. The talks could make no progress afterwards. The government reported that, in 2004, China started building roads in the border areas, leading to repeated protests by the Bhutanese government based on the 1998 Peace and Tranquility Agreement. According to a Bhutanese reporter, the most contested area has been the Doklam plateau. Chinese built a road up the Sinchela pass (in undisputed territory) and then over the plateau (in disputed territory), leading up to the Doka La pass, until reaching within 68 metres to the Indian border post on the Sikkim border. Here, they constructed a turn-around facilitating vehicles to turn back. This road has been in existence at least since 2005. In 2007, there were reports of the Chinese having destroyed unmanned Indian forward posts on the Doklam plateau.

Current position

"Boundary talks are ongoing between Bhutan and China and we have written agreements of 1988 and 1998 stating that the two sides agree to maintain peace and tranquility in their border areas pending a final settlement on the boundary question, and to maintain status quo on the boundary as before March 1959. The agreements also state that the two sides will refrain from taking unilateral action, or use of force, to change the status quo of the boundary." —*Ministry of Foreign Affairs, Royal Government of Bhutan.*

Notwithstanding the agreement, the PLA crossed into Bhutan in 1988 and took control of the Chumbi Valley near the Doklam plateau. There were reports of the PLA troops threatening the Bhutanese guards, declaring it to be Chinese soil, and seizing and occupying Bhutanese posts for extended periods. Again, after 2000, numerous intrusions, grazing and road and infrastructure construction by the Chinese were reported as reported in the Bhutanese National Assembly.

INDIA NEEDS TO TAKE CHINESE THREAT AT DOKLAM SERIOUSLY

Is China preparing for another confrontation with India at the Doklam trijunction? Recent reports using satellite imagery suggest a build-up of military infrastructure on Chinese territory less than 100 metres from where Indian soldiers continue to maintain vigil at the trijunction on Bhutanese territory.

Alarmist reports

In official briefings the Indian government has downplayed the Chinese build-up. The fortifications are on Chinese territory. There has been no attempt to encroach upon sovereign Bhutanese land which Indian troops are guarding at Bhutan's behest. Reacting to alarmist reports of a massive military infrastructural build-up near the Doklam plateau, the ministry of external affairs (MEA) said:

"The government would once again reiterate that the status quo at the face-off site has not been altered. Any suggestion to the contrary is inaccurate and mischievous." There is a constituency in India that periodically raises alarmist bogeys over threats, internal and external. In the past, routine army movements near Delhi have been called potential "coups" with rarely used front-page eight-column headlines which are employed by newspapers only for extremely critical events. The coup was not. It was a figment.

The Chinese threat at Doklam though is not an idle one. It needs to be taken seriously. Chief of army staff (COAS) general Bipin Rawat has for some time now been emphasising the Chinese factor in India's overall military preparedness. He says India must shift its tactical military focus from Pakistan to China.

At last week's global Raisina Dialogue, General Rawat, commenting on the presence of China's PLA troops in the north Doklam area, observed: "They have carried out some infrastructure development, most of its is temporary in nature. But while their troops may have returned and the infrastructure remains, it is anybody's guess whether they would come back there, or it is because of the winter they could not take their equipment away. But then we are also there. In case they come (back), we will face them."

The Indian army commander who oversaw the successful disengagement of Indian and Chinese soldiers at Doklam last August after a 73-day standoff has clear views on the current situation on the Line of Actual Control (LAC). Lt General Abhay Krishna heads the Eastern Command which monitors the LAC. In a recent interview, General Krishna said emphatically: "The readiness and reactions of the Indian Army to the Doklam standoff have given courage to India's friendly neighbours to live up to their shared concerns. The situation is now normal with our stand having been clearly articulated, backed up by the readiness of the Army for any security scenario in the forthcoming season."

Elite group

Meanwhile, the successful pre-induction trial of Agni V, an inter-continental ballistic missile (ICBM) with a range of over 5,000 km, places India close to joining an elite group of countries - the United States, Russia, Britain, China and France - that have nuclear-armed ICBM strike capability.

Following one more pre-induction trial, Agni V will be inducted into India's triservices Strategic Forces Command (SFC). Agni V's strike range covers the entire territory of China. An Indian ICBM with a range of 10,000 km -similar to Chinese ICBMs which have a range of up to 14,000 km - is under development. The acquisition of an advanced air defence missile shield, the S-400 Triumf from Russia that can destroy enemy missiles at a range of 400 km and an altitude of 30 km, is in the final stages of negotiations.

Beyond military preparedness on both the Pakistani and Chinese borders, India must use nuanced but robust geopolitics to strengthen its neighbourhood strategy. Towards this end, the United States and India will hold their first "two-plus-two" dialogue in April 2018. It will feature the defence and foreign ministers of the two countries: Nirmala Sitharaman and Sushma Swaraj for India and general James Mattis and Rex Tillerson for the US.

GROWING ENGAGEMENT

China is wary of the growing diplomatic and military engagement between Washington and New Delhi. Its spokesmen have "warned" time and again that the US-India strategic partnership should not be aimed at countering China's "inevitable rise", as Beijing puts it, and global influence. China was incensed by being described as a "disruptive, transitional force in the Indo-Pacific" by Admiral Harry Harris who heads the US Pacific command. Beijing sees the emerging "quad" alliance between the US, India, Japan and Australia as an impediment to its ambitions in the South China Sea as well as a spoke in its Belt and Road Initiative (BRI) that will give it seamless access to the markets of Africa, the Middle East and Europe.

India's membership of the Australia Group, finalised last week, in addition to its earlier entry into the Wassenaar Arrangement and the Missile Technology Control Regime (MTCR) - non-proliferation groups that China is not a member of - will not worry Beijing much. The three groups are obligation-oriented regimes. China's objective is to block India from the Nuclear Suppliers Group (NSG) which is rights-based. But since the other three groups that control the spread of nuclear, chemical and biological weapons have common members with the NSG, China's obsessive opposition to India's membership will be increasingly untenable.

Not a single shot has been fired along the LAC between Chinese and Indian soldiers for over 40 years. That tranquillity, despite China's military build-up in Doklam, is likely to continue. But as General Rawat says coldly, if they come, "we will face them."

INDIA-CHINA RIVALRY EXPOSED IN ONGOING BORDER DISPUTES

As a consequence, the 4,056-kilometer (2,520 miles) frontier between India and China, one of the longest inter-state borders in the world, remains the only one of China's land borders not defined, let alone demarcated, on maps or delineated on the ground. While Indians doubt China's sincerity in border negotiations, Chinese question India's leaders' will and capacity to settle the dispute in a "give-and-take" spirit. Up until 2005, there was a great deal of optimism about a possible breakthrough. Evidence of this came during Prime Minister Vajpayee's China visit in June 2003 when New Delhi's readiness to address Chinese concerns on Tibet was matched by Beijing's willingness to resolve the Sikkim issue by recognizing the trade route through the Nathu La Pass on the China-Sikkim frontier with India and later showing Sikkim as part of India in its maps.

For its fraction, New Delhi reiterated its stance on the Tibetan Autonomous Region as part of China. This visit also paved the way for border talks to be held through special representatives of the leaders to find an early "political solution" to the boundary question, rather than going only by the legal and historical claims of the two sides. India indicated its willingness to settle for the territorial status quo by giving up claims to the Aksai Chin in Ladakh and hoped China would give up its claims to Arunachal Pradesh in the eastern sector and recognize the McMahon Line just as Beijing had accepted Tibet's British-drawn boundaries with Afghanistan and Myanmar (formerly known as Burma).

In order to give a new thrust to the ongoing border negotiations, an "Agreement on the Political Parameters and Guiding Principles for the Settlement of the Boundary Question" was signed during Chinese Prime Minister Wen Jiabao's visit to India in April 2005. The joint statement issued at the end of the visit talked of a "Strategic and Cooperative Partnership" between India and China.

No Group

Since then, though, Beijing has upped the ante by demanding major territorial concessions in populated areas of Arunachal Pradesh on terms that many in New Delhi see as "humiliating and non-negotiable." Tawang, in particular, has emerged as a sticking point since the Chinese claim it to be central to Tibetan Buddhism given that the sixth Dalai Lama was born there. Ties between China and India were strained even further in May 2007 when the Chinese government refused a visa to an Indian official from disputed Arunachal Pradesh to visit China, and the Indian government's invitation soon thereafter to Taiwan's opposition Kuomintang (K.M.T.) party presidential candidate, Ma Ying-jeou, to visit India in June 2007 to hold talks with senior Indian officials. China voiced its opposition to Ma's visit and called on India to abide by the "One

China policy." Thereafter came media reports of the People's Liberation Army (P.L.A.) encroachments across the Line of Actual Control (L.A.C.) and Chinese small arms supplies to insurgents in India's volatile northeast via Bangladesh and Myanmar. Then, in August 2007, Beijing demanded the removal of two old Indian Army bunkers near the tri-junction of Sikkim, Bhutan and Tibet, claiming that these were located on their territory. This move raised questions about China's declared policy of treating Sikkim as part of Indian territory. Not surprisingly, China's increasing assertiveness over the disputed borders has led to a rapid meltdown in the Sino-Indian border talks and a "mini-Cold War" has quietly taken hold at the diplomatic level during the past two years, despite public protestations of amity.

Some observers argue that Hu Jintao's desire to control the choice of the next Dalai Lama has led to pressuring India to concede access to the Tawang Monastery, which is crucial to this choice. The deterioration in Sino-Indian relations under Hu, however, should not have come as a surprise given his reputation as a hardliner over Tibet. (After all, Deng Xiaoping had groomed him for the Chinese Communist Party leadership because of his prominent role in the successful suppression of the Tibetan revolt in 1988.) In this context, the rapid pace development of road, rail and military infrastructure in Tibet close to its borders with India and Nepal is seen as preempting any possible destabilization of Tibet post-Dalai Lama. Others, however, do not see any sinister designs in western China's development.

Instead, they attribute the recent downturn in Sino-Indian relations more to domestic power struggles within the Chinese Communist Party (C.C.P.) than to the Dalai Lama succession issue or to Chinese concerns about India's growing tilt toward the United States. While there may be an element of truth in all these arguments, there are other more fundamental reasons behind the recent chill in Sino-Indian relations. Apparently, the strategic consequences of India's economic resurgence coupled with U.S. Secretary of State Condoleezza Rice's offer in March 2005 to "help make India a major world power in the 21st century" have greatly bothered the Chinese. This offer, and the long-term India-U.S. defense cooperation framework and the July 2005 U.S.-India nuclear energy deal that followed soon after, have been compared by Chinese strategic analysts to "the strategic tilt" toward China executed by former U.S. President Richard Nixon in 1971 to contain the common Soviet threat. Claiming that these developments have "destabilizing" and "negative implications" for their country's future, China's India-watchers have started warning their government that Beijing "should not take India lightly any longer."

Chinese leaders be led to believe that China's growing economic and military might would eventually enable Beijing to re-establish the Sino-centric hierarchy of Asia's past as the U.S. saps its energies in fighting small wars in the Islamic world, Japan shrinks economically and demographically while India remains subdued by virtue of Beijing's "special relationships" with its South Asian neighbours. However, a number of "negative developments," from Beijing's perspective, since early 2005 — the Indian and Japanese bids for permanent seats on the U.N. Security Council, the formation of the East Asia Summit that includes India, Australia and New Zealand, the Indo-U.S. nuclear deal, India's ability to sustain a high economic growth rate of eight to nine percent and the strategic implications of India's "Look East" policy — have apparently upset Chinese calculations.

Therefore, after a hiatus of a few years, Chinese media commentaries have resumed their criticism of Washington's "hegemonic ideas" and for drawing "India in as a tool for its global strategic pattern." Some Chinese analysts express serious reservations about U.S. efforts to draw "India in as a tool for its global strategic pattern," arguing that "India's DNA doesn't allow itself to become an ally subordinate to the U.S., like Japan or Britain."

Nonetheless, most see India as a "future strategic competitor" that would be an active member of an anti-China grouping due to the structural power shifts in the international system and advocate putting together a comprehensive "contain India" strategy based on both economic tools (aid, trade, infrastructural development) and enhanced military cooperation with "pro-China" countries.

NEGOTIATING STRATEGIES

One repeated emerging criticisms of India's negotiating strategy is that "unilateral concessions" have been made too often by India, without similar concessions being made by China. When PRC military forces started moving into Tibet in 1950, the Republic of India quickly moved to (a) give up the Forward Rights inherited from the days of British India, which stemmed from the Simla Convention and Anglo-Tibetan Agreement of 1904; and (b) instead recognise Chinese control over Tibet in stronger terms than the hitherto used term "suzerainty". In effect, a "Tibet Card" was there to be played at a time of PRC uncertainties. A robust Indian intervention might have maintained Tibet as an effective buffer between India and China, or at least enabled concessions to be won by India on the Himalayan—Karakoram borders. This is the reverse logic behind recent Indian comments that "China has failed to appreciate that if Arunachal is claimed to be the southern part of Tibet Autonomous Region (TAR), India cannot accept Tibet to be within China. India's formal position on Tibet articulated in 1954 and 2003 is therefore a tentative and unilateral diplomatic offer that can only be sustained and the circle completed once China recognizes Arunachal as part of India". Reinvoking such a "Tibet Card" has been floated in some Indian circles in the past few years.

Having lost that opportunity, the next criticism of Indian negotiating strategy is that, faced with an immediate PRC military presence in Tibet and renewed Chinese claims over Aksai China and Arunachal Pradesh, Nehru ignored the chance of a trade-off seemingly offered by China in 1960; whereby Aksai China would have gone to China and Arunachal Pradesh would have gone to India. Instead, India refused to engage in sovereignty negotiations in the 1950s, maintained its claims to the fullest, neglected to build up its own military forces, yet still engaged in adventurist forward probing movements in the late 1950s. At the time, Nehru rejected the idea of territorial trade-off; India "will not concede one piece of territory in return for another in the same manner as a similar dispute between China and Burma was settled this year"; for "there is no question of barter in these matters ... facts are facts". His formal position was, in the formal *Indian Note* of June 16 1962; quite simply that "this boundary is well known and well recognized and has been so for centuries and cannot be the subject of any negotiations". The trouble was the precise boundaries were not well known, were not well recognized, and had not been in shape for centuries. The irony is that the territorial agreement reached between Burma and China in 1960 involved China following the MacMahon Line alongside other mutual concessions and swapping of territory; as did the 1963 Agreement between China and Pakistan with regard to mutual concessions over claims and territory in the Karakoram reaches.

Nehru might have said "facts are facts" but the fact of the matter is that China's military superiority and continuing occupation of Aksai Chin created a very different subsequent set of facts in the wake of India's military defeat at the hands of China in 1962. The problem for consideration of negotiated resolution of the territorial dispute is that demands and offers have shifted. From the outside, an obvious trade off would be between the *Western* Sector and the *Eastern Sector*; which is where Noorani argued that "there is no territorial dispute which has been, and still is, more susceptible to a solution than India's boundary dispute with China. Each side has its non-negotiable vital interest securely under its control. India has the McMahon Line; China has Aksai Chin" In other words, China's *de facto* control of Aksai Chin could be reflected in agreed *de jure* sovereignty for China, and India's *de facto* control of Arunachal Pradesh could in turn be reflected in agreed *de jure* sovereignty for India. This had been Zhou Enlai's seeming suggestion in 1960, and was the "Package Plan" floated by Deng Xiaoping during 1980. The problem is that the Indian government has never taken up such trade-off offers, with Chinese comments made about the weakness of the Indian governments in taking any compromise deal to the Indian public. The separate *sector-by-sector* approach advocated by India when discussions resumed in the 1980s, rather than *overall package* trade-off deals suggested by China, has not worked, it has merely led the PRC to maintain its particular claims in all Sectors.

Another possible example of unilateral concessions was Rajiv Gandhi's visit to Beijing in 1988. Various concessions were made by him. He agreed that the settlement of the border dispute no longer was necessary as a precondition for improvement of bilateral relations, secondly he agreed that some members of the Tibetan community in India were engaged in anti-China activities, and thirdly he agreed that Tibet was an internal affair for China. Ganguly considered the results were "clearly asymmetric" as no support on the Kashmir issue was received from China, which "underscored the stark debility of India's negotiating capabilities vis-à-vis China". On the other hand, the earlier unequivocal support for Pakistan's case in Kashmir was moderated by a more neutral position by the 1990s, the PRC eventually announcing it was "not taking sides on Kashmir".

A final example of "unilateral concessions" came in the 2003 *Declaration on Principles for Relations and Comprehensive Cooperation between India and China*, in which India explicitly recognised the sovereignty of China over Tibet. A careful look at the text shows one-way agreement, one-way obligations, one-way concessions. On the one hand, it stated that "The Indian side recognizes that the Tibet Autonomous Region is part of the territory of the People's Republic of China and reiterates that it does not allow Tibetans to engage in anti-China political activities in India"; before going on to immediately say, on the other hand, "The Chinese side expresses its appreciation for the Indian position and reiterates that it is firmly opposed to any attempt and action aimed at splitting China and bringing about "independence of Tibet". As can be seen, there was no recognition of Indian territory (Arunachal Pradesh?) by China; not even return recognition by China of India's sovereignty claims over Sikkim, the Princely State reincorporated into the Republic of India in 1975, an incorporation which China had refused to recognise. Indian commentators may have read the accompanying *Trade Memorandum* designating Natu La as a border trade post as recognition by China of India's sovereignty over Sikkim, but that was implied rather than explicit, *de facto* rather than *de jure*.

Meanwhile, New Delhi has refused to lay out its formal position, other than the reiteration of its full claims of the Indian Parliament in November 1962, a unanimous vote to get China to vacate all Indian-claimed territories that China occupied. Specific territorial negotiations involving sensitive political climb downs or concessions might well be conducted in private out of the public gaze, yet there seems no indications of this either. India could then indicate some sort of territorial trade-off, short of this maximalist reiteration of its full claims which China is unlikely to accept. Of course, India indicating a territorial trade-off would not necessarily meet with Chinese acceptance, given Indian suspicions that China is happy enough to avoid definitive frontier settlement; but at least it would clarify the issue, and in such an eventuality enable India to more straightforwardly strengthen her own presence and power towards China along the border. In IR terms, if *engagement* proved unsuccessful in leading to territorial settlement, then India could go for a degree of*internal balancing*through building up its military presence and power in Arunachal Pradesh and Ladakh. Some Indian commentators have suggested that "when the Agni-III is finally ready for deployment, it is likely that the Chinese will come down to the table for negotiations and there is likely to be further progress on the border dispute". It could also go for a degree of *external balancing* with others vis-à-vis China but that is a much wider issue. It could try adjusting its bigger policy on Tibet, in effect playing a "Tibet Card" to engineer geopolitical shifts in the future; though would be a much more high risk strategy immediately bringing it up against China's perceived "core interest" of averting internal fragmentation.

If India's strategy over the disputed territories has been hesitant, this has been exacerbated by the very opaqueness, the "Chinese whispers" coming from Beijing. What exactly does China really want, what is its bottom line? For example, are PRC reiterations of claims over the whole of Arunachal Pradesh, re-invoked with greater vigour since the 1990s, just a maximalist initial tactic to end up with the Tawang pocket, thereby strengthening its control over Tibet, a line of argument by Chinese commentators like Ma Jiali and others. Are some suggestions in PRC circles of a different trade-off, Aksai Chin to India and Arunachal Pradesh to China, serious?

Did China's acceptance in 2003 of Nathu La as an official border trade post between India and China represent full and definitive acceptance by China of Sikkim's incorporation into India; and what is the significance of rising "incursion" incidents into Sikkim during 2008 by Chinese troops; uncertainties that undermine Wen Jiabao's assertions in 2005 that "Sikkim is no longer the problem between China and India?"

Is talk in the PRC that "China won't make any compromises in its border disputes with India" a tactical ploy by China to get India to make compromises? If it is, then a trade-off deal is likely at some point. If it is not, then indefinite deadline/ stand off is likely, unless one or the other disputant state attempts to decide it on the military battlefield.

One emerging line from the PRC, with implications for India, is PRC emphasis and definition of a "core interests" diplomacy, reflecting the rise of China; "as the country becomes stronger, China is now on the trajectory to develop its own doctrine of diplomacy".

This has been a development in the last couple of years, overlapping with rising friction along the disputed Himalayan reaches; generally what the PRC calls "the recalibration of its strategic focus in diplomacy to 'core interests'", over which it is taking a more obstructive/assertive line. This sense of "core interest" can be primarily seen at stake for the PRC in Taiwan and also Xinjiang.

It can also be seen with PRC statements with regard to Tibet, whereby "Tibet related issues remain a core interest of China that refers to state sovereignty and territorial integrity. This is neither a religious issue nor a human right issue". The question is how far China's "core interest" framework may be "expanding". If such a "core interest" linkage is also invoked for Arunachal Pradesh (or in PRC eyes *Zang Nan* "Southern Tibet") as "Tibet-related issues", then one would have less expectations of territorial agreements being reached between India and China, and more likelihood of armed resolution in the future.

Such trends were the spur for Barat Verma at the *India Defence Review* to warn that for the PRC "the most attractive option is to attack a soft target like India and forcibly occupy its territory in the Northeast...Beijing's cleverly raising the hackles on its fabricated dispute in Arunachal Pradesh to an alarming level, is the preparatory groundwork for imposing such a conflict on India"; a scenario dismissed in China as a "provocative and inflammatory illusion". Nevertheless, IR security dilemma dynamics may indeed lead to increasing military tension as both sides reinforce their military positions, and "war talk" about the disputed territories increases.

Concerned voices are easy to find as "tensions over a boundary dispute between the two sides are escalating". One reason for Indian concerns is the increasing number of "incursion" incidents along the border, though denied by China. The official India leadership downplays such trends, India's Foreign Secretary Niripuma Rao thus asserting in September 2009 that "there has been no significant increase in intrusions across all Sectors of the Line of Actual Control (LAC)", but that such India-perceived incursions were "because there is no mutually agreed or delineated border". This ignores the earlier increase the previous year, whereby the number of India-perceived "incursions" by the PRC has increased from 140 in 2007 to 280 in 2008, with a similar number in 2009. Such incursion incidents involved not just the *Eastern Sector* around Arunachal Pradesh but now also the *Western Sector* around Aksai Chin/Ladakh; a particular widening development that Indian commentators like Bhaskar Roy have found "sinister" and which Kanwal sees as "aggressive tactical posturing" on the part of China.

Admittedly, such border incursions, reflecting different perceptions of where the LAC actually is, have often been trivial in themselves; for example Chinese troops painting rocks in red paint or cross-LAC sheep grazing. Chinese troop movements near and around the narrow Siliguri corridor "chicken's neck" linking north-east India to the rest of India do though cause immediate geopolitical concerns to India.

Certainly, a substantive military build up along the Aksai Chin and Arunachal Pradesh borderlines has also been evident. Partly this has been an infrastructure race, in which India has been belatedly trying to catch up and match China's better established road, and now railway, infrastructure in these disputed borderlands.

It has also involved increasing military deployment, again by India to match China's already established forces in places like Linzi airbase. This is reflected in India increasing its ground forces in the border regions facing China. In the *Eastern Sector*, this has also involved the Indian Air Force (IAF) deploying advanced long range Sukhoi Su-30 warplanes to Tezpur for potential cross-LAC operation; complemented by six surface-to-air Akash missile squadrons. In the *Western Sector*, this has also involved the Indian Air Force reactivating disused high altitude airstrips like Daulat Beg Oldi and Fukche. Such reinforcements have been picked up in the PRC, and denounced as "unwise military moves".

Meanwhile, Brahma Chellaney asked the question in 2006 "will India—China border talks ever end"? He argued that "after a quarter century of unrewarding negotiations with

Beijing, India ought to face up to the reality that it is being taken round and round the mulberry bush by an adversarial state that has little stake in an early border resolution"; in which "the more the talks have dragged on, the less Beijing has appeared interested in resolving the border disputes other than on its terms".

His prognosis was simple, "it is time for it to draw the line, at least in the negotiations" and "to re-evaluate the very utility of staying absorbed in a never-ending process". Three years later, in the wake of the 2009 talks, his sense was the same, "the latest round of the unending and fruitless India—China talks on territorial disputes was a fresh reminder of the eroding utility of this process".

The PRC may indeed wish to keep the issue open as a way of distracting and threatening India; but other dynamics may be leading the PRC to postpone decisive border negotiations. The PRC may well consider tightening its hold on Tibet itself as a greater priority, shaken during the disturbances that swept across Tibet and Tibetan areas in the spring of 2008? The PRC may also want to delay decisive border territorial resolution with India until it has resolved the Taiwan issue first? Garver also has wondered how far Beijing's apparent slowdown and readiness to avoid territorial resolution with India, is because of "understanding between Pakistan and China that neither will settle their territorial disputes with India independently of the other". Such a consideration point to the wider Pakistan—China—India triangle interplay around the disputed territories that stretch along the Himalayas from Arunachal Pradesh in the east to Aksai Chin and Kashmir in the west, which overlap with basic power balancing by the China—Pakistan "nexus" against India. The overlaps between the varied territorial disputes was shown in 2009 when China gave visas for the entry of Kashmiri separatists to visit China, in the wake of India giving permission to the Dalai Lama to visit Arunachal Pradesh.

What is certain is that any quick decisive territorial resolution between India and China is unlikely. Following rising border frictions, the PRC media reported "China—India border dispute turns sour", with hard hitting nationalist blogs being noticeable in the Chinese official and state controlled media in the autumn of 2009.

Admittedly, the Indian and Chinese leadership did again reaffirm dialogue in autumn 2009. However, this reaffirmation was in cautious terms "to gradually narrow differences on border issues between the two countries ... to continue talks, with the aim of incrementally removing the barriers to a solution that was fair and acceptable to both sides".

Despite the euphemistic headline from the official Chinese media that the two countries had reached "concensus on narrowing border differences"; in reality this merely indicated the existence of a gap without showing how and when it would be resolved. Talk of "gradually" and "incrementally removing" barriers to a solution flags up the slowness of any likely process, whilst offering nothing on what solutions could then emerge once such barriers have been, incrementally, removed.

What of solutions? Could outside arbitration be one way forward? Nehru himself had offered such a route in the immediate aftermath of war in the shape of the International Court of Justice (ICJ) at The Hague. However this was badly received in Parliament and Nehru then backed away immediately from this. In reality the ICJ seems ill equipped to deal with direct large scale territorial disputes between major powers, whilst China's reluctance to have outside bodies disposing of sovereignty issues is higher even than India's.

One bilateral solution which we can return to, involves a *logic of geography,* the "watershed/crestline" line along the Himalayas/Karakoram. It has a degree of clearness, "the advantage of having a border on such a prominent line as the high watershed of the Himalaya is that it is easily identifiable, historically traditional and politically neutral". It may also be sellable to both parties.

Thus, "as far as the Indian public is concerned, they have been brought up to believe that the Himalaya is the traditional boundary and they will be willing to concede any territory that lies beyond it without demur"; whilst "such a boundary should also be acceptable to China as it is based on the same watershed principle which they have accepted in defining their boundaries with Myanmar, Sikkim and Nepal.

This watershed principle was an angle suggested by Zhou Enlai in the abortive 1960 discussions. In effect, applying the watershed principle would leave Aksai Chin to China and almost all Arunachal Pradesh with India.

Admittedly, Tawang remains problematic. The Tawang District's 2,085 square kilometres is around 2.5% of Arunachal Pradesh's entire 82,743 area, and its population of 38,924 is around 3.6% of Arunachal Pradesh's 1,091,120 inhabitants (2001 figures), relatively small shares on paper.

Neutralization of the entire Tawang subdivision pocket might be an option. Within the Tawang District, given that the Tawang Subdistrict and the District capital Tawang (27°34'47"N) itself lies north of the Se la Pass and the Ka crest line (27°32'26"N), whereas the Lumla and Jang Subdistricts lie on the southerly India-facing slopes of that crest line; could a division of Tawang District be carried out, with the Tawang Subdistrict allocated to China and the Lumla and Jang Subdistricts allocated to India?

However, local opinion at the District capital Tawang, population c. 20,000, would probably vote in favour of staying in 'India' rather than going into the 'PRC', though an independent 'Tibet' option would provide an interesting third option. Having Tawang subdivision inhabitants relocate further south if they wished might be another solution, though ugly in political and human terms. Meanwhile, if the Dalai Lama's death was followed by any proclaimed rebirth at Tawang, a not impossible scenario, the situation would be still more complicated with the PRC.

Failing dramatic regime change scenarios of regime collapse/ democratization in the PRC, and re-establishment of a genuinely autonomous or independent Tibet, and Tawang notwithstanding;

some sort of trade off involving Aksai Chin and Arunachal Pradesh seems the most likely way forward. In using relatively clear cut neutral geographic principles, the deadlocked politics and unclear history could perhaps be sidelined?

Such a trade off would give neither side too much geopolitical advantage, but also ensure a degree of security for each? A *logic of geography* for the future for the national leaderships that would enable these two neighbours to get past the inconclusive divisive *logic of history* between them, and would provide a mutually satisfactory *logic of power* in terms of geopolitical equilibrium outcomes. Failing resolution of their territorial issues, the grinding tectonic plates along the Himalayas will continue to have their geopolitical counterpart as the two Asian giants look at each other across these disputed areas.

6

The Border War

The serious fighting of the 1962 China-India Border War extended from October 10, 1962, until November 20, 1962. While the entire border was the issue, the actual fighting occurred in three widely separated areas: Walong, Tawang, and Aksai Chin.

It is significant that while over 47,000 square miles of frontier were in contention between China and India, that the fighting was confined to areas where the Chinese felt that they had legitimate claims. In Walong, the British (O'Callaghan, in 1914) had moved the previously agreed British and Chinese border markers northward. In Tawang, portions of India's forward policy extended even north of their claim, the McMahon Line. And in Aksai Chin, the Chinese firmly believed that the (1899) MacDonald-Macartney Line had been the accepted boundary for decades. In any case, no official boundary, over the 2,500 miles frontier, had ever been negotiated and established between the two countries.

An Indian patrol of fifty Rajputs had moved to Yumtso La without incident on the evening of October 9th. At daybreak on October 10th, they began to move toward the Yumtso La bridges. Outnumbering the Indians by about 20:1, a full battalion of Chinese emerged from their positions and quickly moved down the ridge, to form for attack. The Indian positions came under fire from heavy mortars. The Indians were able to hold off the first Chinese assault; the Chinese were apparently unaware of the Indian positions covering Tseng Jong village from the flank, and enfilade fire caused heavy Chinese casualties. The Indian commander at Tseng Jong asked for covering fire while he withdrew from what he felt was a hopeless position; but the covering fires were refused. As the Chinese pressed their attack, the Indian force of fifty was ordered to disengage and retreat to the river; engagement at Tseng Jong would have meant disaster for the Indians.

The Chinese allowed them to withdraw, and held their fire as the survivors crossed the bridge to the south. Chinese casualties were 33 killed or wounded. Indian casualties were seven killed, seven missing, and eleven wounded—50% casualties. The Chinese buried the Indian dead with full military honors, in plain view of the retreating Indian comrades withdrawing south of the river.

The brief battle at Tseng Jong would have grave implications. The Chinese had attacked the Indians with force and determination. Most important, Chinese forces had not retired as General Kaul and Prime Minister Nehru had assumed when they formulated their forward policy.

It was now clear to Kaul that capturing Thag La Ridge was out of the question. The Seventh Brigade remained on the Namka Chu, and was even ordered to extend its posts to the western end of the ridge. On October 12th, Nehru confirmed that he had ordered the army to clear the Chinese from Indian territory. But by October 18th, it was evident that the Chinese were making preparations for an attack; their troop and supply buildups provided ample indication of pending assault.

Meanwhile, on October 18th, the Indians were concerned about Tsang Le; Tsang Le was no more than a positon marked by a herdsman's hut at the sourse of the Namka Chu, but it was tactically important as a possible flank approach to the Chinese positions below Thag La Ridge. One Indian company had occupied Tsang Le since early October; the Chinese had promptly dispatched troops to protect against a flank attack. On October 18th, General Kaul ordered two companies to Tsang

Le. Tsang Le, though, was not only north of the McMahon Line, but also was inside Bhutan; the Indian companies were told to ignore the Line and the boundary.1 On the 19th, the two companies prepared to move toward Tsang Le.

On the night of October 19-20, three regiments of Chinese troops prepared and deployed for their assault on the (Indian) Seventh Brigade in the Namka Chu River area. The Indians had expected the Chinese to cross the Namka Chu by one or more of the five bridges, and hence were defending these crossings. But the Namka Chu, running easterly 1 - 2 miles north of the McMahon Line, was fordable; the Chinese generally forded rather than use the bridges. the Chinese struck near Hathung La and at Tsangdhar; but the weight of the Chinese attack was in the center of the river line. Gurkhas on their way to Tsang Le were victims of Chinese artillery. The Indian units fought fiercely against overwhelming odds, but their positions were overrun one by one. By 9 a.m. the Chinese had secured the riverline. Not only had the Chinese readily taken Indian positions, but they also cut Indian telephone lines. The Seventh Brigade quickly lost cohesion as a fighting force, and was granted permission to withdraw.

The Chinese plan was to sieze Tsangdhar and Hathung La, to cut off both escape and possible resupply. The plan had worded perfectly, especially with the massive Chinese advantage in both troops and firepower. The survivors and remnants of Indian troops withdrew back to Tawang, and the Seventh Brigade effectively ceased to exist as a fighting force by October 22nd. And Tsang Le, so important to General Kaul, was ignored by the Chinese, probably because the Chinese maps (like the Indians') showed Tsang Le in Bhutan.

General L. P. Sen, Commander-in-Chief of Eastern Command, flew to Tawang on October 22nd by helicopter. He ordered the remnants of the Indian troops—two infantry battalions and some artillery—to "hold Tawang at all costs." Sen flew back to Tezpur on October 23rd.

Immediately following the Thag La Ridge-Namka Chu River victory, the Chinese developed a three-prong attack. On October

23rd, the three regiments which had defeated the Seventh Brigade had come throug Shakti and were poised ten miles north of Tawang. A second prong had come through Khinezemane and joined with the first force. A third line of advance came dwon through Bum La. Tawang was poorly suited for the defense, and the Indians decided to withdraw. Tawang was evacuated on October 23rd, and the Chinese occupied it—essentially unopposed—on the next day. Indian forces had now withdrawn to Se La, which they planned to reinforce and defend in strength. There were attacks against Indian posts elsewhere along the McMahon Line in the Tawang Tract; these had fallen under varying degrees of pressure.

In the eastern end of NEFA, the Chinese made some probing attacks against Walong on October 24th and 25th. But after October 25th, NEFA fell into a lull, with the majority of Chinese forces paused in Tawang, about ten miles south of the McMahon Line.

Meanwhile, there had been significant fighting in the western sector, in Aksai Chin. On October 20th, simultaneous with the Thag La Ridge attack, the Chinese assaulted Indian posts in Chip Chap Valley, Galwan Valley, and Pangong Lake. The Galwn post had been surrounded by the Chinese in August, and had thence been sup- polied by air. Galwan post was finally attacked and overrun on October 20th; after reporting that the Chinese had begun to shell the post, it was not heard from again. Numerous small posts were soon overwhelmed and the scant garrisons were either captured or killed. The Western Command then recognized the magnitude of the Chinese attack, and many of the small, isolated posts withdrew to the southwest. On October 21st, after heavy fighting, the Chinese took the posts at the north side of Pangong Lake. More posts, including Daulet Beg Oldi, were evacuated; but the Chinese did not approach Daulet Beg Oldi, for it laid south of their claim line. By pulling troops back, General Daulat Singh of the Western Command had methodically and rapidly built up strength to prepare for any further Chinese attacks. By the first week of November, three brigades—each with four infantry battalions—

were organizing under Singh in Leh. In late October, the Eastern Command made numerous changes—in both command and organization—in the Indian forces after the October defeats. Much of the energies of the Eastern Command were absorbed with these personnel moves; instead of organizing forces, these changes only resulted in confusion amongst the Indian troops on the eastern front.

After the Chinese victories in mid- to late-October, there was a two week lull in Chinese military activity. But it was replaced by a flurry of diplomatic activity.

On October 24th, four days after the outbreak of heavy fighting in NEFA and Aksai Chin, Chou sent a letter to Nehru, proposing: 1) a negotiated settlement of the boundary, 2) that both sides disengage and withdraw twenty kilometers from present lines of actual control, 3) a Chinese withdrawal north in NEFA, and 4) that China and India not cross lines of present control in Aksai Chin.

Nehru's reply of October 27th appeared eager to restore peace and friendly relations, but questioned a mutual twenty kilometer withdrawl after "40 or 60 kilometers of blatant military aggression." Nehru proposed, instead, a return to the "boundary prior to 8 September 1962" before any Chinese attacks; only then would India be interested in talks.

Chou's reply came on November 4th, and clarified his intent of "line of actural control." Chou's "line"—the same that he had repeatedly offered since 1959—was simply the Indian-claimed McMahon Line in NEFA and the traditionally claimed MacDonald Line in Aksai Chin.

Simultaneously, external forces began to influence the Border War situation. Russia, India's supporter through the 1950s, was endorsing the Chinese peace proposal. But in early November, Russia was preoccupied with the Cuban Missile Crisis, and paid little attention to the Border War. Without Soviet support, India had courted support from both England and the United States; military supplies from both countries began arriving in early November. The Americans seemed eager to help India against the perceived menace of Communism; Washington also made plans to send a carrier task force to the Bay of Bengal.

The political activities continued. On November 8th, the Indian Parliament proclaimed a state of national emergency and adopted a resolution to "drive out the aggressors from the sacred soil of India." Through the first two weeks of November, China had refrained from any further assaults; Peking obviously wanted a diplomatic resolution. On November 14th, Nehru wrote another letter to Chou, again rejecting Chou's October 24th proposal, and again refuting any Chinese border claims. But the exchanges between the two countries and the external military support to India had produced no movement toward settlement or compromise. On November 14th, the fighting resumed again.

The Indians had withdrawn from Tawang on October 23rd. The initial withdrawls plan was to draw back to Bomdi La, the northermost point which would allow for a logistic buildup. But the withdrawl orders were almost immediately modified to a withdrawal only to, and defense of, Se La. Se La did appear to be a good defensible position: the only road to Bomdi La ran through Se La, Se La Pass dominated the road from Tawang, and there were dominating peaks on both sides of the Pass. At 14,000+ feet altitude, Se La was definitely "high ground." The problem, however, was the altitude: the weather was harsh, Se La was far from supplies in Bomdi La, and the altitude made air drop of supplies quite difficult. Even if Se La was strongly defended, the Indians knew that they must simultaneously prepare to defend Bomdi La, for they now realized that the Chinese were not a road-bound fighting force. The decision to hold Se La committed the Indians to an extended area, from Se La to Bomdi La, over sixty miles of high-altitude, difficult road.

Over the next several days, the Se La-Bomdi La defense began to form. Se La was sporadically supplied by air. The Indian Government had considered tactical air operations against Chinese positions, but ruled out air strikes because of fear of Chinese retaliation. A supply and manpower buildup began in NEFA. But there was no Chinese attack during the first two weeks of November; and when the first new assault came, it was far from Se La.

The Eleventh Brigade of the Second Division took over the Walong sector on October 31st; the Eleventh was the third unit in ten days to be assigned responsibility for Walong (because of the numerous changes in command). The Walong detachment of three infantry battalions was not, however, preparing for a defense. Even though Chinese strength at Rima was estimated at a Division, the Walong force was planning to attack the Chinese on November 14th, Nehru's birthday. General Kaul had planned a "first major success against the enemy" as a birthday present to Nahru.

On November 14th, two companies of the Kumaon battalion, supported by mortars and artillery, launched an assault against a strategic hill held by company of Chinese fire, then stopped fifty yards from the crest, exhausted. A Chinese night counter-attack cleared the Indians off the hill. The survivors— less than half the attacking force—returned to Walong. The Chinese followed the retreating Indians and penetrated the main Indian defences. Indian artillery could not assist the defense; all rounds had been used in the attack on the Chinese hill. Key defensive points were overrun, and a withdrawal was ordered at 10 a.m. on November 16th. But many of the Indian troops did not receive the order, and fought to the death at their positions. The remnants of the Walong brigade withdrew down Lohit Valley; even in withdraw, many died either from amushes or from privation. The Chinese did not pursue the retreating troops further. The withdrawing General Kaul sent a rather frantic message to New Delhi:

The enemy strength is now so great and his overall strength so superior that you should ask the highest authorities to get such foreign armed forces to come to our aid as are willing to do so.... it seems beyond the capability of our armed forces to stem the tide of the superior Chinese forces which he has and will continue to concentrate against us to our disadvantage. This is not a counsel of fear, but facing stark realities. Only hours after the Walong defeat, fighting would resume in both Aksai Chin and Se La.

In Ladakh, the Western Command continued a steady buildup of forces. By mid-November, a brigade was in place at Chushul (Chusul). Some of the forces were at Chushul village and airport, west of the Chinese claim line. Some of the Indian defences were to the east of the claim line; in fact, the forces east of Chushul were the only Indian forces left in Chinese-clamed territory in Aksai Chin; all other Indian posts in Chinese-claimed territory had been either withdrawn or wiped out. Western Command had made Chushul key terrain as a blocking point between the Chinese and the city of Leh. It is notable that the positions around Chushul were at 14,000-16,000 feet altitude: there was no wood for fires or for constructing bunkers, frozen ground had to be blasted for entrenchments, and even acclimatized troops could work only for short periods. Yet, some strong Indian positions were in place by November 17th. Chinese reconnaissance patrols were visible east of Chushul in mid-November, but no fire was exchanged. On November 17th, a strong Chinese force moved westward toward Chushul. And in the early hours of November 18th, Chinese artillery opened fire on Indian outposts. Mortars and rockets also softened the Indian entrenchments. The Chinese attempted a frontal infantry attack, but it was repelled. Soon, though, the Chinese moved to envelop the Indian positions. In heavy fighting, the Chinese rear and flank attacks were successful. The casualties were heavy for the Indians; one company had only three survivors—the remainder was found fronzen as they died weapons in hand. The Chinese suffered heavy casualties, too. Five hours into the attack, the Chinese had overrun, or forced the evacuation of, every Indian position east of the claim line. The withdrawing Indians regrouped as best they could in the village (and heights behind) Chushul. But the Chinese attack on Chushul village never came; the Chinese stopped at their claim line and did not assault Chushul itself. The War in the western sector was over. Not a single Indian force remained within the Chinese-claimed territory. By the end of November 18th, all of Aksai Chin was in Chinese hands.

In the Se La-Bomdi La sector of NEFA, a steady Indian buildup continued. By November 17th, Fouth Division had ten infantry battalions and some supporting arms—mortars, artillery, and twelve tanks. Concentrated, it could have been a formidable defense; but the force was spread out over the 60 twisty miles of road between Se La and Bomdi La, with the commander and main defences at Se La. Five battalions were at Se La; three, at Bomdi La; and two were at Dirange Dzong*, halfway between. The commander, Brigadier Hosair Singh, soon established his headquarters at the Dzong. Dirang Dzong was poorly suited for defences; but the Indians intended strong defences at Se la and Bomdi La, both of which were well surrounded by hill masses. The defense might have been more successful—if the Chinese had been limited to the road. But there were trails—most notably the Bailey Trail.

Captain F. M. Bailey had explored into Tibet in 1913; his work helped McMahon to draw his boundary line. Bailey had made his way from Tulung La to Lap, and thence through Tse La Pass and southward. The 1962 Indian forces soon came to realize that the Chinese could use the Trail that Bailey had used half a century before. If the Chinese did come down Bailey Trail, they would emerge at Thembang, between Dirang Dzong and Bomdi La. Such a Chinese move would cut off Dirang Dzong and Se La. Yet, despite this, there remained the underlying Indian faith that the Chinese would not attack.

A few blocking forces were sent out in early November: a company to Phutang and a platoon sent up the Bailey Trail to Poshing La. As November advanced, more attention was given to Bailey Trail. Three more platoos—now making a company—were dispatched to Poshing La.

On November 15th, the Chinese—probably a battalion—attacked the company at Poshing La. Radio reports indicated that the Chinese had wiped out the Indian force. But Headquarters could not believe that the Chinese could bring a full battalion down the mountain trail, and a second company from Bomdi La was sent up Bailey Trail. A third company was brought from Bomdi La to Dirang Dzong. By November 16th, the three battalions stationed at Bomdi La was cut to half strenght.

The second company sent to Bailey Trail dug in at Tembang (Thembang) on the morning of November 17th. A Chinese force of about 1500 attacked the company soon after midday. The Indians resisted for three hours, inflicting heavy Chinese casualties.

But logistics problems struck again: the Indians began to run out of ammunition. With darkness falling, the Indian company began to withdraw. But in the darkness and in thick vegetation, and orderly withdrawal soon turned into chaotic flight. None of the company returned to Bomdi La; weeks later, stragglers began appearing on the plains to the south. Again the superior strength of the Chinese and the logistic problems of the Indians had lead to another Indian defeat. But now, the Chinese had cut the road between Bomdi La and Dirang Dzong; about 10,000 Indian troops were northwest of the Chinese road block.

There was a brief (and almost the only) bright moment for the Indians on November 17th. Simultaneous with the Bailey Trail action, the Chinese had launched an attack on Se La. But Se La was well defended; between dawn and midafternoon, the Chinese launched five assaults on Se La, and five times they were repulsed. With five battalions plus artillery, the Se La force was strong—until its main supply route was cut off when the Chinese took Thembang.

Were the Indians at Se La to hold and continue defending, supplied by air? Or should the force withdraw, and if so could it break through the Chinese roadblock? Meanwhile, the Headquarters position at Dirang Dzong, pooly defended, was in jeapordy. Brigadier Singh, commander at Se La, requested guidance from General Kaul.

But General Kaul was still flying around the lost battle at Walong. General P. N. Thapar, Chief of Army Staff, and General Sen, Commander in Chief of Eastern Command, were both at Kaul's headquarters. They both declined to give orders or guidance, deferring instead to General Kaul. An urgent operational decision was needed, but it waited until 7:30 p.m. when Kaul returned.

By the time General Kaul returned that evening (November 17th), there were reports that the Chinese had begun an enveloping movement at Se La and threatened to cut the road between Se La and Dirang Dzong. After a half hour meeting of the three highest ranking officers of the Indian Army, General Kaul issued his order: all units were to pull back from Se La and Dirang Dzong to Bomdi La.

But immediate further discussions amongst the generals resulted in a modification to Kaul's order. The highlights of the new order were as follows:

> You will hold on to your present positions to the best of your ability. When the position becomes untenable I delegate the authority to you to withdraw to any alternative position you can hold.... You may be cut off by the enemy.... Your only course is to fight it out as best you can.

The wording of this order hardly constituted clear guidance.

General A. S. Pathania, commander of 65 Brigade at Dirang Dzong, ordered a withdraw to the plains to the south. Going through Phutang, he himself withdrew. He had hurriedly ordered his tanks to try to fight through to Bomdi La; if the crews could not, they were to abandon their tanks and head for the plains.

But no one took command of the force—two infantry battalions, some tanks, some artillery, and headquarters personnel—left at Dirang Dzong. A few field grade officers (who did not know that withdrawal was ordered) attempted to organize the forces and fight toward Bomdi La. But Chinese forces and ambushes quickly ended the attempt. The survivors straggled southward to the plains. General Pathania would resign soon after the ceasefire. Good control was maintained over the initial withdrawal from Se La; the Indians cleared the first Chinese found behind Se La. But ahead, the Indian column came under heavy machine gun fire. Attempts to knock out Chinese gun positions failed; the road was impassable. Under heavy Chinese fire, the retreating troops headed chaotically south for the plains. In their retreat, many were killed or captured.

By mid-morning of November 18th, the 48 Brigade—six rifle companies at Bomdi La—was the only Indian Army force left in NEFA. The six companies were dug into defensive positions that had been designed for three battalions. They had artillery and mortars, and were expecting reinforcements.

But poor command/control/communications again struck the Indians. At 11 a.m., General Kaul—not knowing that Dirang Dzong was now abandoned—ordered a mobile column (at Bomdi La) to move out to reinforce Dirang Dzong. Brigadier Singh protested that such a move would weaken Bomdi La. But Kaul angrily ordered tow infantry companies, with tanks and artillery, to move out onto the winding road to Dirang Dzong. Support personnel—cooks and clerks—were ordered to aid in the defense of Bomdi La.

The Chinese attacked about ten minutes after the column left. The first attack was beaten off. The infantry in the column was quickly ordered back to their defensive positions; but these were already occupied by the Chinese, and the Indians were caught in the open. A second, stronger Chinese assault followed. Many Indian positions were overrun, and the Chinese brought fire onto the Brigade headquarters; attempts to counterattack failed. By 4 p.m., Singh ordered a withdrawal to Rupa, eight miles to the south.

The Brigade began to organize a defense around Rupa on the night of Novemeber 18th. Then, Singh received orders from IV Corps to withdraw to Foothills, just above the plains. As he began his withdrawal, he received orders from General Kaul to defend Rupa! Turning back, he found that the Chinese were already taking up positions around Rupa; thus, defense of Rupa was impossible. His 48 Brigade was then ordered to Chaku, the next defensible position down the road. The Chinese harrassed the withdrawing troops, and then broke contact. The Brigade, now only one battalion in size, reached Chaku on the evening of November 19th. The Chinese struck at midnight, on three sides. The Chinese had attacked an ammunition supply train, and burning vehicles illuminated the Indian defensive positions. The Brigade broken, scattered groups made their way southward to the plains. Remaining Indian command elements were headed far to the south.

With the disintegration of 48 Brigade at 3 a.m. on November 20th, no organized Indian military force was left in NEFA (nor in Aksai Chin). Militarily, the Chinese victory was complete, and the Indian defeat absolute.

Late on the evening of November 20th, prime Minister Nehru made an urgent and open appeal to the United States for armed intervention against the Chinese; he asked for bomber and fighter squadrons to begin air strikes on Chinese troops in Indian territory "if they continued to advance" and cover for Indian cities "in case the Chinese air force tried to raid them." An American carrier was dispatched toward the Bay of Bengal; but the aircraft carrier was ordered back on November 21st. The victorious Chinese had ordered a ceasefire effective midnight, November 21, 1962.

EVENTS LEADING TO THE SINO-INDIAN WAR

A long series of events triggered the Sino-Indian War in 1962. According to John W. Garver, Chinese perceptions about the Indian designs for Tibet, and the failure to demarcate a common border between China and India (including the Indian Forward Policy) were important in China's decision to fight a war with India.

Numerous changes occurred in the late 1940s. With the independence of the Republic of India and the separate Islamic Republic of Pakistan's creation in 1947, and the establishment of the People's Republic of China (PRC) in 1949. One of the most basic policies for the Indian government was that of maintaining cordial relations with China. The Indian government wished to revive its ancient friendly ties with China. When the PRC was declared, India was among the first countries to give it diplomatic recognition.

After coming to power, the PRC announced that its army would be occupying Tibet. India sent a letter of protest to China proposing negotiations on the Tibet issue. The newly formed PRC was more active in posting troops to the Aksai Chin border than the newly formed Indian republic was. India decided to take moves to ensure a stable Indo-Chinese border. In August 1950, China expressed its gratitude to Indian attempts to "stabilize the Indo-Chinese border". To clear any doubts or ambiguities, Prime Minister Nehru stated in Parliament in 1950 that "Our maps show that the McMahon Line is our boundary and that is our boundary...we stand by that boundary and we will not let anyone else come across that boundary". China expressed no concerns at these statements.

By 1951, China had extended numerous posts in Aksai Chin. The Indian government, on the other hand, concentrated its military efforts on stopping Ladakh from being taken by Pakistani troops and did not establish itself in Aksai Chin. On various occasions in 1951 and 1952, however, the government of China expressed the idea that there were no frontier issues between India and Chinese Tibet to be worried about.

Later, in September 1951, India declined to attend a conference in San Francisco for the conclusion of a peace treaty with Japan because China, which India viewed as an important factor in this treaty, was not invited because of its status as an international pariah. In the coming years India strove to become China's representative in world matters, as China had been isolated from many issues. India vigorously pressed, since the start of the 1950s, for the PRC to be included within the UN.

The People's Liberation Army defeated the Tibetan army in a battle at Chamdo in 1950 and Lhasa recognized Chinese sovereignty over Tibet in 1951. The Indian army asserted control of Tawang at this time, overcoming some armed resistance and expelling its Tibetan administrators. In 1954, the China and India concluded the Five Principles of Peaceful Coexistence under which India acknowledged Chinese sovereignty in Tibet. Indian negotiators presented a frontier map to the Chinese that included the McMahon Line and the Chinese side did not object. At this time, the Indian government under Prime Minister Nehru promoted the slogan *Hindi-Chini bhai-bhai* (India and China are brothers).

- By allowing the Chinese to *take possession* of *Lhasa*, the *Prime Minister* has practically helped them bring their border down to the Indian border... Aggression might well be committed by people who are always in the habit of committing aggression.— B. R. Ambedkar in the Indian Upper House, 1954

On July 1, 1954 Nehru wrote a memo directing that the maps of India be revised to show definite boundaries on all frontiers, where they were previously indicated as undemarcated. The new maps also revised the boundary in the east to show the Himalayan hill crest as the boundary. In some places, this line is a few kilometres north of the McMahon Line. These new maps also revised the maps to show the countries of Bhutan and Sikkim as part of India.

Beginning in 1956, the CIA used Indian territory to recruit Tibetan guerrillas to fight Chinese troops, with a base in Kalimpong, India. The Indian public was outraged when it learned in 1958 that China had built a road between Xinjiang and Tibet through Indian territory in Aksai Chin (historically a part of Indian state of Ladakh).

In 1956, Nehru expressed concern to Zhou Enlai that Chinese maps showed some 120,000 square kilometres of Indian territory as Chinese. Zhou responded that there were errors in the maps and that they were of little meaning. He stated that the maps needed revising from previous years where such ideas were considered to be true. In November 1956, Zhou again repeated his assurances that he had no claims based on the maps.

Tibet disagreements

According to John W. Garver, Nehru's policy on Tibet was to create a strong Sino-Indian partnership which would be catalyzed through agreement and compromise on Tibet. Garver believes that Nehru's previous actions (befriending China on such issues as war in Korea, the PRC's U.N. admission, the peace treaty with Japan and transfer of Taiwan to the PRC, Indochina, and decolonization and the Afro-Asian movement) had given Nehru a confidence that China would be ready to form an "Asian Axis" with India. Much misunderstanding between the two nations led to diplomatic spats over Tibet, with Nehru's move to accommodate the Dalai Lama overshadowing his other actions and opinions on Tibet, including the opinion that an armed resistance movement in Tibet would be suicidal and counterproductive. While China treated India's concerns with Tibet as expansionist, Some in India claim that its concerns were in fact sentimental and culturally-linked, as Buddhist Tibet had been under influence of Indian culture for many years.

Top PRC leader Mao Zedong was humiliated by the reception the Dalai Lama obtained in India when he fled there in March 1959. The Tibet disagreements heightened in the Chinese media, with Mao himself asking Xinhua News Agency on 19 April to produce commentary on unknown Indian expansionists operating in Tibet.

Mao decided on April 25 to openly criticize Nehru for his Tibet policy:

- "Be sharp, don't fear to irritate him [Nehru], don't fear to cause him trouble. Nehru miscalculated the situation believing that China could not suppress the rebellion in Tibet and would have to beg India's help. — Mao Zedong addressing a Politburo Standing Committee

Tensions steadily increased between the two nations when Mao implied that the Lhasa rebellion in Tibet was caused by Indians. On 6 May 1959, Mao published "The Revolution in Tibet and Nehru's Philosophy" where he accused Nehru of openly encouraging Tibetan rebels. This publication was evident of China's perception of India as a threat to its rule of Tibet, which became an underlying reason for triggering the Sino-Indian War. India had become the imperialist enemy, with Nehru and his "big bourgeoisie" striving to "prevent China from exercising full sovereignty over its territory of Tibet" to form of a buffer zone. On the same day, Zhou Enlai lashed out at Nehru's "class nature"."Nehru and people from the Indian upper class oppose reform in Tibet, even to the extent of saying that reform is impossible...[They want] Tibet to remain for a long time in a backward state, becoming a 'buffer state' between China and India. This is their guiding mentality, and also the center of the Sino-Indian conflict. — Zhou Enlai

India continued negotiations about Tibet. According to the Indian official history, India wished to express goodwill to China and stop the claims of it having a hostile design in Tibet. In August 1959, the Chinese army took an Indian patrol prisoner at Longju, which falls north of the McMahon Line coordinates drawn on the Simla Treaty, signed in 1914, map (27°44'30"N), but claimed by India to lie directly on the McMahon Line. There was another bloody clash in October at Kongka Pass in Aksai Chin in which 9 Indian frontier policemen were killed. Recognizing that it was not ready for war, the Indian Army assumed responsibility for the border and pulled back patrols from disputed areas.

On October 2, Nikita Khrushchev defended Nehru in a meeting with Mao. The Soviet Union's siding with Nehru, as well as the United States' influence in the region, gave China the belief that it was surrounded by enemy forces. On 16 October, General Lei Yingfu reported on Indian expansionism on the Thag La Ridge. On 18 October, the Chinese government approved the PLA's plan of a "self-defensive counterattack" against India because of its actions in Tibet.

However, Mao decided against further escalation because he feared that India would retaliate by permitting the U.S. to station U-2 surveillance aircraft on its territory. This would allow the CIA to photograph China's nuclear test site at Lop

Nor in Xinjiang. A few days after Kongka Pass, Chinese Prime Minister Zhou Enlai proposed that each side withdraw 20 kilometres from a "Line of Actual Control". He defined this line as "the so-called McMahon Line in the east and the line up to which each side exercises actual control in the west". Nehru responded with a proposal to turn the disputed area into a no man's land.

Chinese studies of the 1990s still maintain that India was planning aggression in Tibet. Most Chinese scholars believe that the root cause of the war was India's plan to seize Tibet and turn it into a protectorate or colony of India. The official Chinese history of the war states that Nehru was planning to create a "great Indian empire". It was also insisted that there were right wing nationalist forces that influenced Nehru to pursue the goal of controlling Tibet. Zhao Weiwen, of the Chinese Ministry of State and Security, places emphasis on Nehru's "dark mentality". China's policy on Tibet did much to heighten the conflict and tensions between the two nations. The perceptions of India as a capitalist expansionist body intent on the independence of Tibet to create a buffer zone between India proper and China was fundamentally erroneous. The negative rhetoric led to what Zhou himself called the Sino-Indian conflict. Because of these false fears, China treated the Indian Forward Policy of the 1960s, which India admits as a fundamental mistake, as the beginning of Indian expansionism into Tibet.

Border negotiations

China's 1958 maps showed the large strip of land between Ladakh and Bhutan (the Aksai Chin) as Chinese. In 1960, Zhou Enlai proposed that India drop its claim to Aksai Chin and China would withdraw its claims from NEFA. According to John W. Garver, Zhou's propositions were unofficial and subtle. Zhou consistently refused to accept the legitimacy of India's territorial claims; he proposed that the any negotiations had to take into account the facts on the ground. Zhou tried many times to get Nehru to accept conceding Aksai Chin, he visited India four times in 1960. However, Nehru believed that China did not have a legitimate claim over both of those territories and was not ready to give away any one of them. However, they had different opinions as to the legality of the Simla agreement which eventually led to the inability to reach a decision. Nehru's adamance was seen within China as Indian opposition to Chinese rule in Tibet, as China needed the highway through Aksai Chin to maintain an effective control over the Tibetan plateau.

According to Neville Maxwell, Nehru wasn't ready to simply concede the territory and leave negotiations at that. He was open to continued negotiations, but did not accept the idea of Indian troops withdrawing from their claimed regions. Nehru stated "*We will negotiate and negotiate and negotiate to the bitter end. I absolutely reject the approach of stopping negotiations at any state.*" He remained firm that there would be no boundary negotiations until Chinese troops withdrew from Aksai Chin and areas south of the British McMahon Line. This was unacceptable to the Chinese, which never recognized the legal validity of the McMahon Line. Nehru stated "*We will never compromise on our boundaries, but we are prepared to consider minor adjustments to them and to talk to the other side about them.*" In light of these comments, the international community rallied behind Nehru in claiming that China was at fault in failing to conduct proper negotiations. Maxwell argues that Nehru's words were ambiguous.

According to the official Indian history:

- "Nehru did not agree to barter away the Aksai Chin area, under illegal occupation of China, in return for China giving up its unreasonable claim to Indian territory south of the McMahon Line."

After the talks, India produced its official reports on the talks and translated the Chinese report into English. India believed it would improve a feeling of understanding between the nations. China saw it as an unreasonable attempt by India to secure its claim lines. Nehru's adamance that China withdraw from Aksai Chin and thus abandon the highway was seen as further Indian attempts to undermine China's presence in Tibet.

According to John W. Garver, China reached the incorrect conclusion that Nehru was continuing his "grand plans in Tibet".

Forward policy

At the beginning of 1961, Nehru appointed General B.M. Kaul QMG but he was influential in all army decisions. Kaul reorganized the general staff and removed the officers who had resisted the idea of patrolling in disputed areas, although Nehru still refused to increase military spending or otherwise prepare for war. In the summer of 1961, China began patrolling along the McMahon Line. They entered parts of Indian administered regions and much angered the Indians in doing so. After May 1961 Chinese troops occupied Dehra Compass and established a post on the Chip Chap River. The Chinese, however, did not believe they were intruding upon Indian territory. In response the Indians launched a policy of creating outposts behind the Chinese troops so as to cut off their supplies and force their return to China.

According to the Home Minister in Delhi on February 4, 1962:

- "If the Chinese will not vacate the areas occupied by her, India will have to repeat what she did in Goa. She will certainly drive out the Chinese forces."

This has been referred to as the "Forward Policy". There were eventually 60 such outposts, including 43 north of the McMahon Line. Kaul was confident through previous diplomacy that the Chinese would not react with force. According to the Indian Official History, Indian posts and Chinese posts were separated by a narrow stretch of land. China had been steadily spreading into those lands and India reacted with the Forward Policy to demonstrate that those lands were not unoccupied.

India, of course, did not believe she was intruding on Chinese territory. British author Neville Maxwell traces this confidence to Mullik, who was in regular contact with the CIA station chief in New Delhi. Mullik may therefore have been aware of Mao's sensitivity concerning U-2 flights.

The initial reaction of the Chinese forces was to withdraw when Indian outposts advanced towards them. However, this appeared to encourage the Indian forces to accelerate their Forward Policy even further. In response, the Central Military Commission adopted a policy of "armed coexistence". In response to Indian outposts encircling Chinese positions, Chinese forces would build more outposts to counter-encircle these Indian positions.

This pattern of encirclement and counter-encirclement resulted in an interlocking, chessboard-like deployment of Chinese and Indian forces. Despite the leapfrogging encirclements by both sides, no hostile fire occurred from either side as troops from both sides were under orders to fire only in defence.

On the situation, Mao Zedong commented,

- Nehru wants to move forward and we won't let him. Originally, we tried to guard against this, but now it seems we cannot prevent it. If he wants to advance, we might as well adopt armed coexistence. You wave a gun, and I'll wave a gun. We'll stand face to face and can each practice our courage.

Other developments

At a Communist Party conference in Beijing in January 1962, Chinese President Liu Shaoqi denounced the Great Leap Forward as responsible for widespread famine. The overwhelming majority of delegates expressed agreement, but Defence Minister Lin Biao staunchly defended Mao. A brief period of liberalization followed while Mao and Lin plotted a comeback. Jung Chang writes that China was prepared for war with India after the border clashes in May and June, but were concerned about the Nationalists, which had been making active preparations for invasion from Taiwan, and had moved large forces to the south-east coast.

Transcripts from the decision for war was not made by China's leaders until early October 6, 1962, and only then were war plans drawn by China's Central Military Commission. Roderik McFarquhar states, "In May–June 1962, the main concern in Beijing was over the threat of an invasion from Taiwan... Chinese leaders would have been reluctant to provoke hostilities in the Himalayas, which might have meant diverting military resources from the main danger point along the Fujian coast."

The Indian military was not ready for full-scale combat. India had just annexed the Portuguese State of India or, Goa and was facing border disputes with Pakistan in Kashmir. The Indian National Congress proposed non-violent means to solving India's problems, and Indian military leaders, who proposed that India should prepare for a full scale attack, were ignored or dismissed.

Early incidents

Various border conflicts and "military incidents" between India and China flared up throughout the summer and fall of 1962. According to Chinese sources, in June 1962, a minor skirmish broke out between the two sides, and dozens of members of the People's Liberation Army killed and wounded. Units of the Indian and Chinese militaries maintained close contact throughout September 1962; however, hostile fire occurred only infrequently.

On May 2, 1962 the Directorate of Military Operations in India had suggested that the air force should be readied for use in NEFA and Ladakh. The Air Force was considered a feasible way to repel the unbalanced ratio of Chinese troops to Indian troops and the Chinese air force was assessed as only capable of limited strategic raids which could be countered by the Indian air force. Indian Air Force soon started reconnaissance flights over the NEFA border. On May 7, 1962 Chinese troops shot down an Indian Dakota plane in which young officer B. P. Tiwari was lost. Following this incident, the Indian Air Force was told not to plan for close air support.

In June, 1962, the Indian Intelligence Bureau said it received information about a Chinese military buildup along the border which could result in a war. Information was also received that Pakistan was considering to attack simultaneously in the west. Chinese airfields in Tibet and Yunnan were addressed as a threat to Indian cities, as the PLAAF could conduct heavy bombings through their use of Soviet aeroplanes.

On July 8, the Chinese initiated another diplomatic communication, to protest against an alleged Indian incursion into the Galwan Valley. According to China Quarterly, the Government of India released press reports to the public indicating that Indian had gained 2,000 mi^2 of territory from the Chinese. However, in their diplomatic reply to the Chinese, India denied that any incident had taken place.

On July 10, 1962, 350 Chinese troops surrounded an Indian post at Chushul, in the Galwan Valley, north of the MacMahon Line. They used loudspeakers to obtain contact with the Gurkha forces stationed there. The Chinese troops attempted to convince the Gurkhas that they should not be fighting for India, to cause an abandonment of the post. After a fiery argument the 350 Chinese withdrew from the area.

July 22, 1962 saw a change in the Forward Policy, according to the official Indian history of the war. While the Forward Policy was initially intended to prevent the Chinese from advancing into empty areas (by occupying them first), "it was now decided to push back the Chinese from posts they already occupied." Whereas Indian troops were previously ordered to fire only in self-defence, all post commanders were now given discretion to open fire upon Chinese forces if threatened.

In August, 1962, the Chinese military improved its combat readiness along the McMahon Line, particularly in the North East Frontier Agency, Tibet and Xinjiang. In Tibet, there were constructions of ammunition dumps and stockpiling of ammunition, weapons and gasoline, though there were no indications of a manpower buildup. China's preparedness for war strongly contrasted with India's, which had largely neglected its military throughout the 1950s. Nehru believed that the Himalayas were a large enough defence against China, however, the Korean war had provided China with practice in mountain combat. This neglect on behalf of India would decide numerous pivotal battles where logistical inadequacy and lack of leadership led to defeat after strong starts.

Confrontation at Thag La

In June 1962, Indian forces had established an outpost at Dhola, on the southern slopes of Thag La Ridge, overlooking the village of Le in Tibet. Based on the treaty map of the 1914 Simla Convention, the McMahon Line lay at 27°44'30"N. However, Dhola post lay about one mile (1.6 km) north of the McMahon Line The Indian government maintained that the *intention* of the McMahon Line was to set the border along the highest ridges, and that the international border fell on the highest ridges of Thag La, about 3 to 4 miles (4.8 to 6.4 km) north of the line drawn by Henry McMahon on the treaty map. Brigadier John Dalvi would later write of this claim: "The Chinese had raised a dispute about the exact alignment of the McMahon Line in the Thag La Ridge area. Therefore the Thag La-Dhola area was not strictly territory that 'we should have been convinced was ours' as directed by the Prime Minister, Mr. Nehru, and someone is guilty of exceeding the limits prescribed by him." In August, China issued diplomatic protests which accused India of violating even the McMahon Line, and Chinese soldiers began occupying positions at the top of Thag La, north of Indian positions. On September 8, 1962, a 60-strong PLA unit descended from the heights and occupied positions which dominated one of the Indian posts at Dhola. Neither side opened fire for 12 days. Nehru had gone to London to attend a Commonwealth Prime Ministers' Conference and, when told of the act, said to the media that the Indian Army had instructions to "free our territory".

According to the official Indian history, a decision was made on September 9 to evict the Chinese from the southern part of the Thag La Ridge, by force, if necessary. Two days later, it was decided that "all forward posts and patrols were given permission to fire on any armed Chinese who entered Indian territory".

According to author Neville Maxwell, officers at the Indian Defence Ministry had expressed the concern that Indian maps showed Thag La as Chinese territory; they were told to ignore the maps. However, Nehru's directives to Defence Minister V.K. Krishna Menon were unclear, and the response, code named Operation LEGHORN, got underway only slowly. As the Chinese numbers were exaggerated to 600 instead of about 50 or 60, the 9 Punjab battalion, numbering 400 riflemen, was sent to Dhola.

By the time the Indian battalion reached the Thag La Ridge in the Chedong region on September 16, north of the McMahon Line, Chinese units controlled both banks of the Namka Chu River. The day after, India's Chief of the Army Staff Gen P N Thapar ordered his men to re-take the Thag La Ridge. According to the official Indian history, on September 20, Indian eastern command ordered all Indian posts and patrols to engage any Chinese patrols within range of their weapons. On September 20, at one of the bridges on the river a firefight developed, killing nine Chinese and Indian soldiers. Skirmishes continued throughout September. On 3 October, Zhou Enlai visited Nehru in New Delhi, promising there would be no war between the nations and reiterating his wishes to solve the dispute diplomatically. On October 4, a new corp was created 4 corp, under Lt. Gen. B.M. Kaul, tasked with evicting the Chinese from Dhola-Thag La October 10 was the planned date for Operation Leghorn. Because of the difficulties involved in directly assaulting and taking Thag La, Kaul made the decision instead to occupy nearby Yumtso La to the west, to position his troops behind and dominate the Chinese positions.

Brigadier John Dalvi, tasked with taking Yumtso La, argued that he lacked necessary supplies and resources to take the pass. On October 9, Kaul and Brigadier Dalvi agreed to send a patrol of 50 soldiers to Tseng Jong, the approach to Yumtso La, to occupy the position and provide cover before the rest of the battalion would move forward for the occupation of Yumtso La.

On October 10, these 50 Indian troops were met by an emplaced Chinese position of some 1,000 soldiers. The Chinese troops opened fire on the Indians believing that the Indians had intruded upon Chinese land. The Indians were surrounded by a Chinese positions which used mortar fire. However, they managed to hold off the first Chinese assault, inflicting heavy casualties. In the second assault, the Indians began their retreat, realising the situation was hopeless. The Indian patrol suffered 25 casualties, with the Chinese suffering 33. The Chinese troops held their fire as the Indians retreated, and then buried the Indian dead with military honours, as witnessed by the retreating soldiers. This was the first occurrence of heavy fighting in the war.

This attack had grave implications for India and Nehru tried to solve the issue, but by 18 October it was clear that the Chinese were preparing for an attack on India, with massive troop buildups on the border.

THE COMBATANTS: THE CHINESE AND INDIAN ARMIES IN 1962

The Chinese People's Liberation Army (PLA) is the unified organization, under a single command, of all Chinese land, sea, and air forces. The estimated strength of the PLA in 1962 was approximately three million officers and men. The 1962 ground combat forces consisted of about 130 divisions, mostly infantry. China is divided into eleven military regions, including the Sinkiang Military Region—responsible for Aksai China—and Chengtu Military Region—responsible for the northeast Indian border.

Chinese combat power was organized around an Army, with a strength of approximately 4,500 officers and 38,400 soldiers. Each Army has three Infantry Divisions, with a strength of approximately 1,300 officers and 11,300 soldiers in each Division. Major equipment of the Infantry Division included the Light Machine Gun, Antitank Grenade Launcher, and Mortars. Infantry Divisions included three Infantry Regiments, a Tank Regiment and an Artillery Regiment. An Infantry Regiment had three Infantry Battalions, equipped with 7.62mm Assault Rifles and Carbines. Even with China's massive combat manpower available, the nature of the 1962 Border War—mountain and cold weather operations—dictated tactics generally limited to the battalion and company level.

The PLA had both strengths and weakness in its readiness for mountain warfare against India. Perhaps China's biggest weakness was the economic and budgetary constraints on the Army. The Soviets has willingly supplied the PLA in the 1950's. But deteriorating relations—including border disputes—with Russia led to the end of Soviet military aid in 1960. Further, China faced national economic difficulties in the late 1950s and early 1960s. This resulted in progressive cutbacks and constraints from 1960 to 1962 for the PLA: ".... so serious was the shortage of military equipment and materials that it caused trouble in the training program.... The Ground Force is also facing the difficulties of obtaining fuel, ammunition, and batteries for the use of their vehicles and in training." The 1962 Taiwan Strait Crisis put further strains on the PLA's resources. Clearly, the watchword for the PLA was self-reliance—making due with the supplies and equipment that were available. Finally, while there has often been political control of the PLA, there was especially tight central control regarding border incidents; official orders in all border regions stated that ".... under no circumstance should an officer upon his own personal responsibility take steps to carry out an unauthorized decision" regarding any border/international incident; officers were directed to report incidents, and then await decisions and orders.

On the positive side, the PLA was well prepared for mountain warfare in the Himalayas. China had gained extensive experience in both mountain and cold weather warfare in Korea; many Korea verterans were still in the PLA in the early 1960s. Not only had China gained further experience in alpine warfare over the past twelve years in Tibet, but she was fighting in the same area (the Himalayas being the southern frontier of Tibet). The Chinese were acclimitized to the weather and the altitudes. They had outposts, patrols, and military construction (e.g. the two Aksai Chin roads) in the frontier. Further, the Chinese augmented their strength and mobility by using local Tibetan guides. Finally, the PLA was well prepared for this type of warfare. The troops had warm, padded uniforms. They carried only what rations they needed to complete a particular mission. And they trained and practiced mobility, moving through mountain passes or over ridges at night, encircling the enemy. Even their mortars and small artillery was mobile. The Indian soldiers would report that the Chinese burp gun and human wave assaults were "demoralizing."

Despite its defense budget problems, the People's Liberation Army appeared to be prepared and ready for military operations in the Himalayas. The Indian Army's readiness for alpine warfare was quite a different story.

The Indian Ministry of Defense was the central agency for formulating and implementing the government's policy decisions on defense matters. There were three branches of service: army, navy, and air force. The Army was organized into three Commands - Western, Eastern, and Southern. Units from the Eastern and Western Commands would be organized into Corpslevel Border Commands. XXIII Corps was responsible for all of NEFA; within XXXIII Corps, 4 Division was responsible for the McMahon Line. The IV Corps would be formed in September, 1962, to assume portions of the NEFA defense. In the west, XV Corps had responsibility for Aksai Chin.

When India gained her independence in 1947, the Indian components of the British Indian Army were divided between Indian and Pakistan on a ratio of 2:1. The first years of the Indian republic were marked with a generally anti-military attitude; many Indian leaders remembered the role of the army in the bloody civil war that preceeded independence; this helped contribute to pacifistic attitudes. Further, Nehru (and others) minimized foreign threats; in regard to China, Nehru stated that the Himalayas "made an effective barrier." Thus, the 1950s was generally a decade of neglect for the Indian Army. Because India believed that there was no external threat to her—with the exception of Pakistan—the national defense budget was minimal. In the mid-1950s, the Army numbered about 350,000, and there was only minimal growth in manpower over the next several years; after India's 1962 defeat, the Army's numbers would leap to 827,000!

The Indian Army had significant personnel problems. The Army had only eight divisions—seven infantry and one armour. Only three battalions were available to the Western Command in the early 1960s. The budget constraints on the army and India's pacifistic attitude aggravated another problem: the British had provided much of the leadership of the British Indian army; without the British, there was a shortage of experienced officers and NCOs. It was thus difficult to build up military strength, especially when the advice of experienced senior officers was often ignored.

Apparently, Indian intelligence was also lacking. Their lack of preparedness for warfare in the Himalayas would indicate a very poor concept of the topography and weather in the area, resulting in very poor mobility across the mountains. Indian intelligence and reconnaissence seemed ignorant of Chinese strength, mobility and tactics, especially night movements and human wave attacks which the Indians called the "Red Ant Swarm."

The Indians had problems with fire power. Because of limited budget, they had minimal artillery and difficulty keeping it adequately supplied with ammunition. The artillery they did have was often immobile in the mountains.

Another area affected by the budget was training. Technical training was lacking, and there were simply not enough supplies and munitions for adequate training. Worse, there was little training for mountain warfare.

Perhaps the major problem—another result of the limited defense budget—was the logistic one. Even with foreign aid (primarily from Russia), the Indian army was lacking in virtually every area of equipment and supplies. The logistic shortfalls had many serious consequences. India lacked the engineering equipment for alpine operations. They had tentage, but not enought to house even half the soldiers. Rations were often in short supply, resulting in many hungry days for the Indian soldiers. Their communications equipment was minimal. And, almost unbelievably, the Indian army came to the Himalayas (to altitudes above 15,000 feet) in cotton, summer uniforms! Finally, transportation of supplies was a serious problem. Roads into the mountains were few; often, supplies came on long final legs by pack animal. The Indians resorted to supply by air drop, but even this had problems. Aging parachutes were used with supplies, and supplies crashed to the ground often when the parachutes failed. To make matters worse, many of the air drops landed on Chinese, rather than Indian, encampments (and to add insult to injury, the Chinese would throw out the "inedible" Indian rations)!

In summary, the Indian army was in a poor state, especially in their readiness for alpine warfare. Their fire power, supply system, training, and readiness for mountain operations were all quite lacking. They had significant personnel shortages, and would often be outnumbered by the Chinese by 5:1.2 To pit troops in such circumstances against an enemy superior in every detail of military strength would be absurd; to leave them in an early winter of heavy snow and freezing temperatures would be to condemn them to steady and severe attrition from exposure and illness and, before long, starvation. But this is what India did.

Under these circumstances, India's forward policy was militarily nonsensical. But some politicians and leaders simply believe what they want to believe. Nehru was still convinced that his army would be almost invincible against the Chinese. He would soon learn how wrong he was.

SUMMER 1962 SKIRMISHES

Well into 1962, Nehru continued to ignore the advice of his generals about the army's poor state of readiness; he also continued to assume that China would not or could not assert herself against India. Hence, Nehru continued his "forward policy" of furter extending Indian outposts and border patrols. India's purpose was to pursue the forward policy to drive the

Chinese out of any area New Delhi considered hers. On February 4, 1962, the Home Minister declared, "If the Chinese will not vacate the areas occupied by her, India will have to repeat what she did in Goa. She will certainly drive out the Chinese forces." The Indian strategy in early 1962 was to move behind Chinese posts in an attempt to cut off Chinese supplies. China's reaction any new Indian outpost, thought, was usually to surround it with superior forces.

The diplomatic letters and protests continued, usually totally uncompromising and unproductive. In January, both sides accused the other of violating their air space. A February 26th Chinese not suggested that maintaining the status quo of the boundary was the only way to avoid military clashes, and again suggested withdrawing the troops of each side twenty kilometers back. The note concluded with the statement that "the door for negotiations is always open." In fact, China had already stopped all patrols within twenty kilometers of the border. But India again rejected the proposal, and continued to insist that the Chinese withdraw to behind the Indian claim line before there would be any negotiations on the border question. In April, Nehru announced that "We do not want war with China, but that is not within our control. Therefore we have to prepare for the contingency." An April Chinese letter protested Indian intrusions, and demanded that India withdraw from the Karakoram area. On May 14th, the Indians proposed to allow China to "continue to use the Aksai Chin road for civilian traffic" if China would otherwise withdraw from all Indian-claimed territory. China's reply rejected the idea but again stated that it was better to resolve the issue than to fight. In June, the 1954 Trade Agreements, including the Five Principles of Coexistence, expired; talks produced no new trade agreement, and trade representatives returned home. Relations between the two countries continued to deteriorate.

Throughout the early months of 1962, China had several external problems, especially the Taiwan Straits Crisis. Chinese leaders continued to insist that they did not want war, but that Aksai Chin was clearly Chinese and was strategically important to the People's Republic. China began to commit more border patrols—in reaction to increased border activity by Indian troops in Spring 1962. In June, when the Taiwan Strait situation eased, China's attention returned to the border situation and she brought more pressure to bear on New Delhi. India, too, continued to escalate by establishing new outposts to "defend Indian territory from further inroads."

The crisis had brewed for three years. Despite many menacing confrontations and endless protests, there had been very few casualties thus far. But in July this changed.

A Gurkha platoon had been sent forward to cut off Chinese outposts in the Galwan Valley (in Aksai Chin). On July 10th, a Chinese battalion surrounded the Indian post, cutting it off from supplies. The Chinese were attempting to halt Indian advances in Ladakh; but India continued to supply the Galwan Valley outpost by air drop. New Delhi sent a reinforcing force toward Galwan Valley, but it was turned back by the Chinese. India was continuing to move forward in an attempt to pressure China into withdrawing from the disputed area.

On July 21st, there was a skirmish in the Chip Chap Valley. Two Indian soldiers were wounded, the first since Konga Pass in 1959. The Chinese protested, and also accused India of violating the McMahon Line in NEFA. Indeed, General B. M. Kaul, then Chief of the General Staff, had ordered the establishment of 24 posts along the McMahon Line. In June, local Indian commanders had established Dhola Post, in Tawang. The relevant issue was that Dhola Post was one mile north of the McMahon Line, in Chinese territory even by Indian standards. On August 4th, Peking accused India of violating the McMahon Line (at Dhola), and of aggression beyond its own claimed border—and therefore into Chinese territory.

But Chinese pressure was ineffective. On August 14th, Nehru told Parliament that India had three times as many posts in Ladakh as China; Nehru asked for a free hand to deal with China, and Parliament gave it to him. In August, China improved its combat readiness in NEFA, Tibet and Sinkiang.

While there was no sign of a manpower buildup in Tibet, there was construction of ammunition dumps and shockpiling of ammunition, weapons, and gasoline.

On September 8th, the Chinese reacted to the Indian outpost at Dhola. A Chinese patrol of sixty soldiers—which the Indian commander reported as 600—moved over and down the Thag La Ridge, into positions which dominated the Indian post at Dhola. The Chinese patrol suggested that local officials meet to discuss where the border lay. Orders from Nehru refuded any discussions and orders the army to relieve the Dhola Post and force the Chinese back behind Thag La Ridge. A serious clash between the sides ensured. The XXXIII Corps commander, General Umrao Singh, had protested that driving the Chinese back behind the Ridge was militarily nonsensical; Singh was later relieved and replaced by the more compliant General B. M. Kaul. Nehru used the Thag La incident to whip up national and international support. Further skirmished continued through September.

By late September, China had resumed patrols along the entire border. On September 20th, another clash occurred at Chedong, at the junction of India, Bhutan and Tibet. Both sides took casualties, including one Chinese officer killed. The fighting for physical control of disputed land was increasing. There were both Indian and Chinese protests about the Chedong incident: India accused China of expansionism, and China warned that there was a limit to her patience and self-restraint. Unfortunately for the Indians, Chedong was another area where China seems to have had legitimate claim. Many Indians must have questioned India's actions in Chedong, north of the McMahon Line (and Nehru's orders to push the Chinese back even further); pushing military force past India's claimed boundary clearly made India the aggressor in this and some subsequent clashes. Much of the more serious fighting to come in October was not in the areas which both China and India claimed, but in areas (Tawang and Walong) where China had a legitimate claim or where India had pushed beyond the McMahon Line. Sporadic fighting in the Chedong area continued for the next few weeks, suggesting that India was determined to drive Chinese forces back.

Now, India seemed unwilling even to discuss any border issues or proposals. An October 3rd Chinese note suggested a meeting to discuss the entire border was met with a curt Indian refusal. On September 26th, General Kaul assumed command of XXXIII Corps; this Corps was hampered by widely dispursed troop concentrations, few weapons, inadequate supplies, and no winter clothing. On October 5th, India created a special Border Command under the command of General Kaul. Kaul was already in NEFA, preparing an "all out effort" to expel the Chinese from Thag La. On October 9th, General Kaul ordered General John Dalvi, Commander of the Seventh Brigade, to take Yumtso La Pass. Dalvi argued that he lacked the military resources—and the winter clothing—to take the 16,000 foot Pass. Kaul compromised, and sent a fifty man patrol to Tseng Jong. the patrol reached Tseng Jong before dark on October 9th without Chinese resistance. Little did the patrol know that bloody fighting— and the China-India Border War—was only a few hours away.

THE AFTERMATH

The 1962 Debacle, as it is remembered in India, was the inexorable ramification of a century-old British border dispute, thrust upon a newly independent India. When China reached a juncture whence it could act proactively to the sense of injustice about colonial actions against them, the result was an eruption of a xenophobic, aggressive imperialism.

There is a Chinese phrase oft quoted within the Chinese government: "If he strikes me once, it is his fault. If he strikes me again, it is my fault." The People's Republic of China seemed to have taken this mentality to heart, and in the effort to exorcise the demons of colonialism, have become imperialists themselves. Subverting various indigenous countries and areas in affirmation of vague "historical" citings had become a fundamental cornerstone of China's geo-strategic maneuvering in the '50s and '60s.

The Chinese claims to Aksai Chin and large areas of Arunachal are a mix of an expression of this neo-colonial sentiment and the desire to acquire a dominant status in Asia by keeping rival India in a weaker bargaining position. This is not saying that the PRC is necessarily "evil" in this respect, as many Indian journalists are prone to claim; it is simply geopolitics. What is unusual, however, is the rather unscrupulous means, even among the big-power nations, that the PRC has taken to reach this position. When China sought recognition of its claim on Tibet after its occupation, the Chinese leadership avidly cultivated India, and won the heart of a high-minded but naïve Prime Minister Nehru. "Hindi-Chini Bhai-Bhai" (India and China are brothers) became the soundbyte of the day - and the Chinese cannot be faulted in their execution of this deception. While the shells fell and the bullets flew around the Jawans in the snow-capped hell of the Himalayan battlefield, the Indian leaders in Delhi were romancing the fluffy pull of empathy with a fraternal Asian nation that, too, had suffered exploitation by the Western colonial powers.

Added to the chaos and the mounting of tensions after the border clashes and failed settlement talks in 1960, and arguably a prime factor in making the dispute a mutual national prestige issue, was the internal political flux within both India and China. India was democratic and, therefore, more sensitive to its public and parliamentary opinion, and highly politicized debates about the Chinese question raged across the Parliament floor and in stratified governmental agencies. In particular, the elected representatives of the various Communist parties in India were indignant by the notion that their fraternal socialist brethren would be capable of starting such a conflict, and laid the blame solely on the "capitalist-lackey" Nehru's shoulders. At the opposite end of the political spectrum, the right-leaning parties blamed the crisis on a "socialist" Nehru's ignorance and non-recognition of the reality of situation. On the other side, a communist Peking did not have this intra-political problem, but it was engaged in intense ideological remolding and suffered from a sense of political isolation, aggravated by its increasing ideological differences with Russia since 1958, when the latter, for example, refused to give it a sample atom bomb.

The '62 war highlighted several critical failures in India's warmaking abilities. First, and perhaps most significantly, the conflict highlighted political naïveté and ignorance toward the strategies of warfare and international relations. During the entire conflict, Indian diplomatic actions remained flaccid, and fluctuated between being confrontational to being manhandled. For example, intel told that the Chinese were building a road through Aksai Chin, yet the Government, apart from a few angry condemnations, chose to ignore the strategic significance of it for almost a decade, instead repeating to itself the mantra of Hindi-Chini bhai-bhai. Even upon discovery of this transgression, India's protests were weak-kneed. Later, in the middle of 1962, Indian leaders suddenly woke up to the presence of Chinese soldiers, to the exasperation of much of the army, on the Thagla Ridge. Nehru, advised by Krishna Menon and a coterie of sycophantic generals, ordered a reckless operation on the attacking Chinese. In the adoption of a forward policy, against the clamoring of sound tacticians, India deployed on ground chosen for its political significance, rather than tactical defensibility. The leadership's untenable demands on the Army were the root cause of the '62 debacle.

The war also highlighted the fact that the army was acutely under-equipped, out-dated, and ill-trained to deal with sustained conflict in the Himalaya. The acclimatization of troops was of critical import in this mountain war. Though Indian kill ratios were vary favorable, the damage caused by non-acclimatization of troops, particularly in the eastern sector, compared to the troops in Ladakh, who were better equipped and acclimatized, is very evident.

The psychological and political effects of the '62 war were far-reaching. Because of the war, India's image, especially among the "Third World", the nations remaining non-aligned during the Cold War, suffered. But internally, the shock galvanized the people into one united nation. Krishna Menon resigned and Nehru's dream of Sino-Indian friendship was shattered, but

India did not relinquish its independent policy of Non-Alignment, though a shadow was shed on India's position as the leader of the Non-Aligned Movement (NAM). However, statements by the PRC promoting the Chinese revolution as a model and Beijing's actions in the Taiwan Strait in 1958 and the 1962 Sino-Indian War alarmed many Third World nations. During the 1960s China cultivated ties with Third World countries and insurgent groups in an attempt to encourage "wars of national liberation" and revolution to forge an international united front against both the superpowers. Third World appreciation for Chinese assistance coexisted, consequently, with growing suspicions of China's militancy. These increasingly militant tendencies, contradictory to the much lauded "Principles of Peaceful Coexistence" soundbyte, destroyed what active influence the PRC had on the NAM. Discord between China and many Third World countries continued to grow, while relations India and the Soviet Union warmed to counter the decision by Pakistan to cavort to the Western Camp in an effort to counter Indian superiority and influence. The two most powerful nonaligned nations strayed further from their NAM policies, and thus the weakened NAM did not wield as much influence during the later part of the Cold War as it did during the beginning, and thus the era of a strictly bi-polar Cold War world was ushered in.

The Indian Army's defeat by the Chinese in the border war of 1962 was a national humiliation, but the nation reacted to the '62 war with an unprecedented surge of patriotism. The main lesson India learned was that right does not make might in the world of geopolitics, and that India must strengthen its defenses and stand on its own feet to be of consequence in the world. India's policy of weaponization via indigenous sources and self-sufficiency was thus cemented. National sovereignty, it would affirmed, could not come at the expense of becoming a client state of any superpower or by joining any military alliance with or under them.

In the early '80s, following a new paradigm shift in the Indian military, it was decided that the Army was to actively patrol the Line of Actual Control. Friction began to ensue over the Chinese occupation of the Sumdorong Chu pasturage, lying north of Tawang. The media, catching wind of the situation, gave it national prominence, and an angry exchange of official protests between the Indian and Chinese governments followed. Adding to the bickering, a bill was passed creating the state of Arunachal Pradesh, a territory that China claims in its entirety.

The military re-occupied Hathung La ridge, across Namka Chu, twenty-five years after vacating it. Army chief K. Sundarji airlifted an entire brigade to nearby Ximithang, alarming the panicked Chinese. The Indian government collectively flinched against the tough talk from Beijing, but stood firm at the insistence of the army. The result paradoxically was a thaw. In 1993 and 1996, the two sides signed the Sino-Indian bilateral Peace and Tranquillity Accords, an agreement on maintaining peace and tranquillity along the LAC. Ten meetings of a Sino-Indian Joint Working Group (SIJWG) and five of an expert group to determine where the LAC lies have taken place but the pace of progress has been tardy to say the least.

7

China–India Border Doklam Standoff

The 2017 China India border standoff or Doklam standoff refers to the military border standoff between the Indian armed forces and the People's Liberation Army of China over Chinese construction of a road in Doklam near a trijunction border area, known as Donglang, or Donglang Caochang (meaning Donglang pasture or grazing field), in Chinese. On 16 June 2017 Chinese troops with construction vehicles and road-building equipment began extending an existing road southward in Doklam, a territory which is claimed by both China as well as India's ally Bhutan. On 18 June 2017, around 270 Indian troops, with weapons and two bulldozers, entered Doklam to stop the Chinese troops from constructing the road. On 28 August, both India and China announced that they had withdrawn all their troops from the face-off site in Doklam.

BACKGROUND

Doklam is an area disputed between China and Bhutan located near their tri-junction with India. Unlike China and Bhutan, India does not claim Doklam but supports Bhutan's claim. China's claim on Doklam is based on the 1890 Convention of Calcutta between China and Britain, which states in Article I:

The boundary of Sikkim and Tibet shall be the crest of the mountain range separating the waters flowing into the Sikkim Teesta and its affluents from the waters flowing into the Tibetan

Mochu and northwards into other Rivers of Tibet. The line commences at Mount Gipmochi on the Bhutan frontier, and follows the above-mentioned water-parting to the point where it meets Nipal territory.

China asserts that by this Convention, the starting point of the Sikkim-Tibet border is "Mount Gipmochi on the Bhutan frontier" and that this clearly defines the tri-junction point. As per Chinese claims, Doklam is located in the Xigaze area of Tibet, bordering the state of Sikkim. However Bhutan was not a party to the Convention.

In 1949, Bhutan signed a treaty with India giving allowance to India to guide its diplomatic and defense affairs. In 2007, the treaty was superseded by a new Friendship Treaty that replaced the provision that made it mandatory for Bhutan to take India's guidance on foreign policy, provided broader sovereignty but also stated in its Article 2:

In keeping with the abiding ties of close friendship and cooperation between Bhutan and India, the Government of the Kingdom of Bhutan and the Government of the Republic of India shall cooperate closely with each other on issues relating to their national interests. From 1958, Chinese maps started showing large parts of Bhutanese territory as part of China. Localized tensions arose in the 1960s but in the 1970s negotiations between China and Bhutan, with India sometimes playing a supporting role, failed to create a consensus on the status of the Doklam plateau. Bhutan and China have held 24 rounds of boundary talks since they began in 1984, with notable agreements reached in 1988 and 1998, the latter also prohibiting the use of force and encouraging both parties to strictly adhere to peaceful means.

In the early 2000s, China built a road up the Sinchela pass (in undisputed territory) and then over the plateau (in disputed territory), leading up to the Doka La pass, until reaching within 68 metres distance to the Indian border post on the Sikkim border. Here, they constructed a turn-around facilitating vehicles to turn back. This road has been in existence at least since

2005. It is the southward extension of this road that has sparked the 2017 standoff.

Events

On 16 June 2017 Chinese troops with construction vehicles and road-building equipment began extending an existing road southward on the Doklam plateau.

On 18 June 2017, around 270 Indian troops, with weapons and two bulldozers, entered Doklam to stop the Chinese troops from constructing the road.

On 29 June 2017, Bhutan protested to China against the construction of a road in the disputed territory. According to the Bhutanese government, China attempted to extend a road that previously terminated at Doka La towards the Bhutan Army camp at Zornpelri near the Jampheri Ridge 2 km to the south; that ridge, viewed as the border by China but as wholly within Bhutan by both Bhutan and India, extends eastward approaching India's highly-strategic Siliguri Corridor. The Bhutanese border was reportedly put on high alert and border security was tightened as a result of the growing tensions.

On the same day, China Foreign Ministry released a map depicting Doklam as part of China. Using the map as illustration, China's Spokesperson Lu Kang read Article I of the 1890 Convention of Calcutta and asserted that it proved that the Donglang (Doklam) area, a territory North East of Gipmochi as shown on the map, belongs to China.

On 30 June, Ministry of External Affairs of India released the statement entitled *Recent Developments in Doklam Area* stating its official position. It charges China of changing status quo in violation of a 2012 understanding between the two governments regarding finalizing the tri-junction boundary points and causing security concerns, widely understood as at its strategic Siliguri Corridor. It says that "Indian personnel" at Doka La coordinated with Bhutan and "approached the Chinese construction party and urged them to desist from changing the status quo."

On 30 June, answering a question about Bhutan's protest, China's Spokesperson Lu Kang made the following statement about Doklam's history after asserting that the area where the construction activities are underway is totally under the jurisdiction of China because it is completely located on the Chinese side of the China-Bhutan traditional customary line:

Before the 1960s, if border inhabitants of Bhutan wanted to herd in Doklam, they needed the consent of the Chinese side and had to pay the grass tax to China. Nowadays the Xi Zang Tibet Archives still retain some receipts of the grass tax.

On 3 July 2017, China Foreign Ministry Spokesperson Geng Shuang stated that former Indian prime minister Jawaharlal Nehru accepted the 1890 Britain–China treaty:

On September 26 of the same year, when writing back to Premier Zhou Enlai, Prime Minister Nehru unequivocally stated "the boundary between Sikkim and Xi Zang, China was defined by the 1890 Convention. This boundary was demarcated in 1895. There is no dispute over the boundary between Sikkim and Xi Zang (Tibet), China". Indian media reported that Nehru's 26 September 1959 letter to Zhou, cited by China, was in fact a point-by-point refutation of the claims made by the Zhou on 8 September 1959. In the letter, which was accessed by Indian press albeit not published in its entirety, Nehru wrote: This Convention of 1890 also defined the boundary between Sikkim and Tibet; and the boundary was later, in 1895, demarcated. There is thus no dispute regarding the boundary of Sikkim with the Tibet region.

China Foreign Ministry Spokesperson Geng Shuang replied to India media's question about disputed tri-junction with the following comment:

The so-called tri-junction, as the name suggests, is a point. It is not a line, much less an area. India misinterprets tri-junction point as an area, from ulterior motives. This time, the trespassing point of Indian army, is on the Sikkim-China border, which is 2000 metres away from the tri-junction point, Mount Gipmochi, by the 1890 Treaty.

On 5 July 2017, the Chinese government said that it had for the past 24 months a basic consensus with Bhutan that Doklam belongs to China, and there was no dispute between the two countries. On 19 July 2017, China renewed its call for India to withdraw its troops from Doklam.

On 24 July 2017, Chinese Foreign Minister Wang Yi told reporters that it is very clear who is right and who is wrong in the standoff in Doklam, and that even senior Indian officials have publicly said that Chinese troops have not intruded into Indian territory. "In other words, India admitted that it has entered Chinese territory. The solution to this issue is simple, which is that they behave themselves and withdraw," Wang said.

On 2 August 2017, the Chinese foreign ministry released a 15-page official position statement *The Facts and China's Position Concerning the Indian Border Troops' Crossing of the China-India Boundary in the Sikkim Sector into the Chinese Territory*. According to this document, there were still over 40 Indian troops and one bulldozer in Doklam (Donglang) region. Beijing accused India of using Bhutan as "a pretext" to interfere and impede the boundary talks between China and Bhutan. The report referred to India's "trespassing" into Doklam as a violation of the territorial sovereignty of China as well as a challenge to the sovereignty and independence of Bhutan. China says in the 15-page document that it notified India regarding its plan to construct road "in advance in full reflection of China's goodwill".

On 3 August 2017, China charged with four reasons that "India is certainly not for peace" though it always puts peace on its lips.

On 4 August 2017, The Ministry of External Affairs of India refused to confirm or deny when asked why, if India received notification from China in advance on its plan to construct road, it had not used diplomatic channels before sending its troops across the border since it was asking for diplomatic solution.

On 8 August 2017, Chinese diplomat Wang Wenli claimed that Bhutan had conveyed to China through diplomatic channels that the area of the standoff is not its territory, saying, "After the incident, the Bhutanese made it very clear to us that the place where the trespassing happened is not Bhutan's territory." On the next day, the Bhutanese government denied this, saying over the phone "Our position on the border issue of Doklam is very clear" and referring to the governments 29 June statement.

On 15 August 2017, several Indian and Chinese soldiers were alleged to have been injured after a melee broke out between them when a group of Chinese soldiers were alleged to have attempted to infiltrate across the border near Pangong Lake into Indian controlled territory in Ladakh. An Indian intelligence officer said the confrontation occurred after Indian soldiers intercepted a Chinese patrol that veered into Indian-held territory after losing its way apparently due to bad weather.

On 16 August 2017, the state run news agency released a segment of its show "The Spark" on Twitter racially attacking India, the video named the "Seven Sins of India" portrayed a stereotypical Indian with a turban and beard and a typical Indian accent, the segment spoke of Indians having "thick skin" and "pretending to sleep" on the matter of the border standoff between the two countries. The video went on to claim India was physically threatening Bhutan, and compared India to a "robber who breaks into a house and does not leave". The content of the video were factually incorrect. The video has received strong backlash on Twitter as well as from the international media.

On 9 October 2017 China announced that it is ready to maintain peace at frontiers with India reacting to Indian Defence Minister Nirmala Sitharaman's visit to Nathu La.

BHUTANESE REACTIONS

After issuing a press statement on 29 June, the Bhutanese government and media maintained a studious silence. *The Bhutanese* clarified that the territory on which China was building a road was "Bhutanese territory" that was being claimed by China, and it is part of the ongoing border negotiations. It also defended the policy of silence followed by the Bhutanese government, saying "Bhutan does not want India and China to go to war, and it is avoiding doing anything that can heat up an already heated situation." However, *ENODO Global*, having done a study of social media interactions in Bhutan, recommended that the government should "proactively engage" with citizens and avoid a disconnect between leaders and populations. ENODO found considerable anxiety among the populace regarding the risk of war between India and China, and the possibility of annexation by China similar to that of Tibet in 1951. It found a strengthening of Bhutanese resolve, identity and nationalism, not wanting to be "pushovers".

The New York Times said that it encountered more people concerned about India's actions than China's. It found expressions of sovereignty and concern that an escalation of the border conflict would hurt trade and diplomatic relations with China. ENODO did not corroborate these observations. Rather it said that hundreds of Twitter hashtags were created to rally support for India over China and that there was a significant blowback over the *Xinhua* video "7 sins". Scholar Rudra Chaudhuri, having toured the country, noted that Doklam is not as important an issue for the Bhutanese as it might have been ten years ago. Rather the Bhutanese view a border settlement with China as the top priority for the country. While he noticed terms such as "pro-Chinese" and "anti-Indian" often used, he says that what they mean is not well-understood.

Disengagement

On 28 August 2017, India and China announced that they had agreed to pull their troops back from the face-off in Doklam. By the end of the day, it was reported that the withdrawal was completed.

The Indian troops withdrew back to their original positions at their outpost at Doka La, located in a militarily advantageous position on the Bhutanese border, less than 500 meters away down the ridge slope. *The Times of India*, citing a source, reported: "Our soldiers sit on the top, hold the ridge and can swiftly intervene, as they pro-actively did in mid-June, if the People's Liberation Army once again tries to unilaterally change the status quo by constructing a road near the Sikkim-Bhutan-Tibet tri-junction."

Ministry of External Affairs (MEA) of India released a press statement stating that India and China had mutually agreed to disengage. It said that India and China had maintained diplomatic communication in recent weeks and that India was able to convey its "concerns and interests".

In Beijing, the foreign ministry spokeswoman said that the Chinese forces on site have verified that the Indian troops pulled out, and implied that Chinese troop numbers would be reduced. She said that the Chinese troops would continue to patrol the area, to garrison it and to exercise "sovereign rights". However, she made no mention of road-building activities. The statement from the Chinese Foreign Ministry spokesman, as *The Diplomat* reported, "offered Beijing a face-saving way out of the impasse." Indian MEA issued a second statement later in the day that both the sides have withdrawn "under verification". The Indian news channel NDTV reported that, by the end of the day, Chinese road-building equipment was removed from the face-off site. Some experts warned that one shouldn't be overly optimistic as another standoff is entirely possible.

The Washington Post commented that it was not clear if China had offered any concessions in return for the Indian withdrawal, such as agreeing to halt road construction. It said that the deal allowed both sides to save face. However China was continuing to be "cagey" in its official remarks. *Al Jazeera* said that China was not giving up its historical claims and it expected India to respect its "historical borders". Scholar Taylor Fravel pointed out that there are plenty of options available to China to garrison the area other than extending the road.

On 29 August, Bhutan welcomed the disengagement and hoped that it would lead to the maintenance of peace and tranquility as well as status quo along the borders.

On 5 September, Prime Minister Narendra Modi and President Xi Jinping held hour-long discussions on the sidelines of the BRICS summit. They agreed on a "forward-looking" approach and vowed to make efforts to ensure that situations like the Doklam standoff do not recur. They reaffirmed that maintaining peace and traniquillity in the border areas was essential for the relations between the two countries.

On 7 September, some media reports claimed that both nation's troops still were patrolling the area at the face-off site, simply having moved 150 meters back from their previous position.

BHUTAN-CHINA BORDER NEGOTIATIONS

470 out of Bhutan's 1,075-kilometer border are adhered to China and the rest 605 to India. Bhutan was once the bridge between Tibet and the east part of South Asia, and shares intimate religious, political, economic, and cultural bonds with Tibet. The Tibetan people cross the Himalayas along the Manas Chhu in east Bhutan and Paro Valley in west Bhutan to Assam, Bangladesh, and Bihar for religious, cultural, and trade activities. The twice-per-year bazaar fair in Bumthang, east Bhutan is a huge attraction for many Tibetan people. The Tibetan caravans offer wool, brick tea, edible salt, and musk in exchange for Bhutan's rice, paper, and dried pepper. Local governments of Tibet deploy officials in areas near Bhutan to purchase rice. It has been a ritual for Tibetans to travel a long distance along the Manas Chhu to embark on pilgrimage at monasteries near Guwahati, Assam. The influx of Tibetan refuges forced Bhutan to close its border with China in 1959, shutting down all cross-border trade activities. No formal trade or commercial relations has been established between Bhutan and China since then.

As a large part of Bhutan-China border is unclear, the focus on China-Bhutan relationship is to resolve border dispute. Border issues between Bhutan and China used to be incorporated into China-India border discussions. In 1959, then

PRC Premier Zhou Enlai issued a letter to India Prime Minister Jawaharlal Nehru expressing China's wish to stage direct bilateral talk with Bhutan. The letter suggests Zhou's intention to separate China-Bhutan border issue from China-India border negotiations. Yet direct border negotiations between China and Bhutan did not begin until 1984. Since then, the capital cities of Beijing and Thimphu have been taking turns hosting the annual border negotiations. By 2004, 17 rounds of talk had been conducted, with the 17th round being held in Bhutan.

Core issues in China-Bhutan border disputes are as follows:

In the 10th round of border talk held in 1996, China proposed to exchange 495 sq km area of Pasamlung and Jakarlung valleys in the northern borders of Bhutan for Sinchulumpa, Dramana and Shakhtoe with an area of 269 sq km in the northwest Bhutan, which share borders with Sikkim, India, but no final decision was taken.

The 12th round held in Beijing in December 1998 centered on establishment of diplomatic and trade relations and ended with the signing of the Agreement between PRC and Kingdom of Bhutan on Peace and Stability in China-Bhutan Border Areas. The five-article agreement demands mutual respect and equal status regardless of the territory and power of a nation. In the agreement, China states its complete respect for Bhutan's independent status, sovereignty, and territorial integrity. The first article provides basis for friendly and good neighbourly cooperation between the two under the five principles of peaceful coexistence. It is understood between the two that differences in border issues had been alleviated and guiding principles for border issue settlement had been established through friendly negotiations in the previous 11 rounds based on the spirit of mutual understanding, mutual trust, and cooperation. The talks have deepened mutual understanding and strengthened traditional friendship between the two, and China and Bhutan are willing to strive together toward the shared objective of settling border disputes in fair and reasonable ways as soon as possible under the principles above. China and Bhutan hereby agree to maintain the status quo of the border as prior to March 1959 and ensure peace and stability of border region before a final solution is reached, and oppose unilateral efforts by either side to change the status quo. As for the progress in the last 11 rounds of border talk, as both sides have made clear their stance, both hereby agree to resolve the issue through friendly negotiations.

While both sides agreed on the need to maintain peace and stability in border region, no final decision was taken on territory exchange. The King of Bhutan once nodded his head on territory exchange in 1997. China again offered the above-mentioned 495 sq km area in the northern border of Bhutan in exchange for the 269 sq km in the northwest Bhutan. The talks came to a halt when the subject of territory exchange was raised. However, following the signing of agreement, Beijing immediately responded to the issues of mule routes and lumber exploration in Pasamlung, and assisted the Tibetan after they were harshly punished by Bhutanese border security troops in Pasamlung for entering Bhutan to collect Tibetan medical herbs. At that time, China was a little bit displeased with Bhutan's mentioning of new issues following years of border negotiations, and therefore agreed to let Bhutan's specialists determine the territory boundary and draw the map of both countries' territories, and also agreed to the use of standard names for areas under dispute to avoid confusion. The King of Bhutan once told the National Assembly that there are 4 areas under dispute, starting from Doklam in the west, along Gamochen at the border, to the river divide at Batangla and Sinchela, and down to the Amo Chhu River.

(1) Up to 89 sq km in Doklam are under dispute.

(2) Approximately 180 sq km in Sinchulumpa and Gieu are under dispute. The border line stretches from Langmarpo Zam along the river up to Docherimchang, through the river divide to Gomla, along the river divide to Pangkala, and finally down to the Dramana River.

(3) Starting from Dramana, along the border line up to Zingula, and along the line of river divide down to Gieu Chhu River, and finally to Lungkala

(4) Starting from the middle of Pasamlum, along the border line and the river divide to Dompala and Neula, going from Neula along the border line and the river divide to Kurichhu Tshozam, along the river divide to Genla then to Mela, and go all the way to the east.

By 1999 China and Bhutan had yet to resolve their border disputes. China sent delegation to Bhutan to carry on with border talks and managed to settle most of the major border disputes. The talks ended satisfactorily for both sides and China, for the first time, expressed their wish to provide financial assistance to Bhutan.

The 14th round of negotiation held in December 2000 saw Bhutan extending their border line further on the one provided by the China government. Bhutan also suggested that technical discussions between experts from both sides be held using maps. In July of the following year (2001), the King of Bhutan said to the National Assembly that border between Bhutan and China should stretch further along Doklam, Sinchulumpa and Dramana. The King also expressed faith that the border dispute between a small nation of Bhutan and a powerful, friendly nation of China would come to a successful settlement in the near future.

Several official interactions between China and Bhutan took place in 2001. The Bhutanese cultural delegation visited China in April, in July the Bhutanese delegation visited Beijing to conduct border talks, and in November the 15th round of border talk was held in Thimphu, capital of Bhutan. However, no final decision was reached with regard to the 3 places (Doklam, Sinchulumpa and Dramana) in question.

In July 2002, the Bhutanese Minister of Foreign Affairs revealed to the National Assembly that China had claimed to be in possession of the license of ownership of the 3 places. Bhutan asked China to extend the generosity of a superpower to a small country like Bhutan, but China replied that it cannot afford to be generous to every single neighbor considering that it has 25 other neighbours. Both sides agreed in the 16th round held in Beijing in October of the same year to create a mechanism in which the border would be examined by map experts from both sides.

No border talk was held in 2003. The 17th round, held in Thimphu in April 2004, saw both sides agreeing to assemble a team of specialists as soon as possible to examine the border. Both sides expressed wish to determine the border as soon as possible and decided to assemble a team of experts to examine the border as proposed by each.

Mutual visits continued, though not on a regular basis. During his visit to Bhutan in April 2003, Hua Junduo, PRC Ambassador to India, reiterated China's friendly, good neighbourly stance toward Bhutan. While there is no formal diplomatic ties between Bhutan and China, said Hua, the relationship is developing in a positive way, and actual relationship is more important than formal diplomatic ties.

Of all countries in Asia and China's neighbouring countries, Bhutan is the only one that has yet to establish formal diplomatic ties with China, preferring to keep a cautious distance from this powerful neighbor. The lack of formal ties has never affected Bhutan's support for China on the international scene. Examples of support include casting a vote in 1971 to keep China's place in the United Nations, inviting the PRC Ambassador to India to the coronation ceremony of King Wangchuck in 1974, speaking repeatedly in favour of China in the United Nations Human Rights Council meetings since 1995, and speaking against Taiwan's bid to host the 2002 Asian Games and the bid to join United Nations. Since 1979, leaders of both sides have been exchanging congratulatory messages on each side's National Day. In the 17th round of border talk held in 2004, King Wangchuck, during his meeting with head of Chinese delegation Wang Yi, reiterated Bhutan's friendly stance toward China, complimented China on its successful reform and opening up, and thanked China for its friendly and good neighbourly stance toward Bhutan. The King also pledged Bhutan's support for China in issues related to China's sovereignty such as Taiwan, human rights, and Tibet.

THE BORDER BETWEEN CHINA AND TIBET

China took advantage of this period of instability in Tibet to seize the regions of Amdo and Kham, making them into the Chinese province of Qinghai in 1724. Three years later, the Chinese and Tibetans signed a treaty that laid out the boundary line between the two nations. It would remain in force until 1910. Qing China had its hands full trying to control Tibet. The Emperor sent a commissioner to Lhasa, but he was killed in 1750. The Imperial Army then defeated the rebels, but the Emperor recognized that he would have to rule through the Dalai Lama rather than directly. Day-to-day decisions would be made on the local level.

Era of Turmoil Begins

In 1788, the Regent of Nepal sent Gurkha forces to invade Tibet. The Qing Emperor responded in strength, and the Nepalese retreated. The Gurkhas returned three years later, plundering and destroying some famous Tibetan monasteries. The Chinese sent a force of 17,000 which, along with Tibetan troops, drove the Gurkhas out of Tibet and south to within 20 miles of Kathmandu.

Despite this sort of assistance from the Chinese Empire, the people of Tibet chafed under increasingly meddlesome Qing rule. Between 1804, when the Eighth Dalai Lama died, and 1895, when the Thirteenth Dalai Lama assumed the throne, none of the incumbent incarnations of the Dalai Lama lived to see their nineteenth birthdays.

If the Chinese found a certain incarnation too hard to control, they would poison him. If the Tibetans thought an incarnation was controlled by the Chinese, then they would poison him themselves.

Tibet and the Great Game

Throughout this period, Russia and Britain were engaged in the "Great Game," a struggle for influence and control in Central Asia. Russia pushed south of its borders, seeking access to warm-water sea ports and a buffer zone between Russia proper and the advancing British. The British pushed northward from India, trying to expand their empire and protect the Raj, the "Crown Jewel of the British Empire," from the expansionist Russians.

Tibet was an important playing piece in this game. Qing Chinese power waned throughout the eighteenth century, as evidenced by its defeat in the Opium Wars with Britain (1839-1842 and 1856-1860), as well as the Taiping Rebellion (1850-1864) and the Boxer Rebellion (1899-1901).

The actual relationship between China and Tibet had been unclear since the early days of the Qing Dynasty, and China's losses at home made the status of Tibet even more uncertain. The ambiguity of control over Tibet lead to problems. In 1893, the British in India concluded a trade and border treaty with Beijing concerning the boundary between Sikkim and Tibet.

However, the Tibetans flatly rejected the treaty terms. The British invaded Tibet in 1903 with 10,000 men, and took Lhasa the following year. Thereupon, they concluded another treaty with the Tibetans, as well as Chinese, Nepalese and Bhutanese representatives, which gave the British themselves some control over Tibet's affairs.

Thubten Gyatso's Balancing Act

The 13th Dalai Lama, Thubten Gyatso, fled the country in 1904 at the urging of his Russian disciple, Agvan Dorzhiev. He went first to Mongolia, then made his way to Beijing. The Chinese declared that the Dalai Lama had been deposed as soon as he left Tibet, and claimed full sovereignty over not only Tibet but also Nepal and Bhutan. The Dalai Lama went to Beijing to discuss the situation with the Emperor Guangxu, but he flatly refused to kowtow to the Emperor.

Thubten Gyatso stayed in the Chinese capital from 1906 to 1908. He returned to Lhasa in 1909, disappointed by Chinese policies towards Tibet. China sent a force of 6,000 troops into Tibet, and the Dalai Lama fled to Darjeeling, India later that same year.

The Chinese Revolution swept away the Qing Dynasty in 1911, and the Tibetans promptly expelled all Chinese troops from Lhasa. The Dalai Lama returned home to Tibet in 1912.

Tibetan Independence

China's new revolutionary government issued a formal apology to the Dalai Lama for the Qing Dynasty's insults, and offered to reinstate him. Thubten Gyatso refused, stating that he had no interest in the Chinese offer. He then issued a proclamation that was distributed across Tibet, rejecting Chinese control and stating that "We are a small, religious, and independent nation." The Dalai Lama took control of Tibet's internal and external governance in 1913, negotiating directly with foreign powers, and reforming Tibet's judicial, penal, and educational systems.

The Simla Convention (1914)

Representatives of Great Britain, China, and Tibet met in 1914 to negotiate a treaty marking out the boundary lines between India and its northern neighbors. The Simla Convention granted China secular control over "Inner Tibet," (also known as Qinghai Province) while recognizing the autonomy of "Outer Tibet" under the Dalai Lama's rule. Both China and Britain promised to "respect the territorial integrity of [Tibet], and abstain from interference in the administration of Outer Tibet."

China walked out of the conference without signing the treaty after Britain laid claim to the Tawang area of southern Tibet, which is now part of the Indian state of Arunachal Pradesh. Tibet and Britain both signed the treaty. As a result, China has never agreed to India's rights in northern Arunachal Pradesh (Tawang), and the two nations went to war over the area in 1962. The boundary dispute still has not been resolved.

China also claims sovereignty over all of Tibet, while the Tibetan government-in-exile points to the Chinese failure to sign the Simla Convention as proof that both Inner and Outer Tibet legally remain under the Dalai Lama's jurisdiction.

The Issue Rests

Soon, China would be too distracted to concern itself with the issue of Tibet. Japan had invaded Manchuria in 1910, and would advance south and east across large swaths of Chinese territory through 1945.

The new government of the Republic of China would hold nominal power over the majority of Chinese territory for only four years before war broke out between numerous armed factions. Indeed, the span of Chinese history from 1916 to 1938 came to be called the "Warlord Era," as the different military factions sought to fill the power vacuum left by the collapse of the Qing Dynasty.

China would see near-continuous civil war up to the Communist victory in 1949, and this era of conflict was exacerbated by the Japanese Occupation and World War II. Under such circumstances, the Chinese showed little interest in Tibet. The 13th Dalai Lama ruled independent Tibet in peace until his death in 1933.

The 14th Dalai Lama

Following Thubten Gyatso's death, the new reincarnation of the Dalai Lama was born in Amdo in 1935. Tenzin Gyatso, the current Dalai Lama, was taken to Lhasa in 1937 to begin training for his duties as the leader of Tibet. He would remain there until 1959, when the Chinese forced him into exile in India.

INDIA AND CHINA AGREE TO END BORDER STANDOFF

India and China have agreed to an "expeditious disengagement" of troops in a disputed border area where their soldiers have been locked in a stand-off for more than two months, India's foreign ministry said on Monday. The decision comes ahead of a summit of the BRICS nations - a grouping that also includes Brazil, Russia and South Africa - in China beginning on Sunday, which Indian Prime Minister Narendra Modi is expected to attend.

Indian and Chinese troops have been confronting each other at the Doklam plateau near the borders of India, its ally Bhutan, and China, in the most serious and prolonged standoff in decades along their disputed Himalayan border. The Indian ministry said the two sides had agreed to defuse the crisis following diplomatic talks.

"In recent weeks, India and China have maintained diplomatic communication in respect of the incident at Doklam," the ministry said in a statement.

"On this basis, expeditious disengagement of border personnel at the face-off site at Doklam has been agreed to and is on-going," it said in a statement. It did not offer more details of the terms of disengagement from the area which had raised fears of a wider conflict between the Asian giants who fought a brief border war in 1962. China said Indian troops had withdrawn from the remote area in the eastern Himalayas. Chinese foreign ministry spokeswoman Hua Chunying said Chinese troops would continue to patrol the Doklam region.

"China will continue to exercise sovereignty rights to protect territorial sovereignty in accordance with the rules of the historical boundary," she said. The Chinese defense ministry said troops would remain on a state of alert. "We remind the Indian side to learn the lesson from this incident, earnestly respect the historical boundary and the basic principles of international law, meet China half way and jointly protect the peace and tranquillity of the border region," spokesman Wu Qian said in a statement.

"The world is not peaceful, and peace needs to be safeguarded. The Chinese military has the confidence and the ability to protect the country's sovereignty, security and development interests," Wu added.

SMOOTH SUMMIT

The trouble started in June when India sent troops to stop China building a road in the Doklam area, which is remote, uninhabited territory claimed by both China and Bhutan. India said it sent its troops because Chinese military activity there was a threat to the security of its own northeast region.

But China has said India had no role to play in the area and insisted it withdraw unilaterally or face the prospect of an escalation. Chinese state media had warned India of a fate worse than its crushing defeat in the war in 1962. Indian political commentator Shekhar Gupta said there was too much at stake for the two countries to fight over a small piece of territory.

"Hopefully, Doklam is a new chapter in India-China relations. Too much at stake for both big powers to let legacy real-estate issues linger," he said in a Twitter post. India and China have been unable to settle their 3,500-km (2,175-mile) frontier and large parts of territory are claimed by both sides.

THE INDIA-CHINA DIVIDE

The Chinese Communist Party's (CCP) dislike for the 'hardline Hindu nationalist' Bharatiya Janata Party (BJP) is no secret. The shifts in India's China policy since May 1998, as evidenced in the nuclear and missile arena, military spending, and pro-Tibet and pro-Taiwan views expressed by some ministers, are said to have undermined the key assumptions underlying China's India policy. Conversations with officials and strategic analysts reveal that the Chinese are concerned over the rise of BJP as a major political force in Indian politics and its implications for China's strategic objective of supremacy in Asia. Before Pokhran II, China's India-watchers had convinced themselves that there would be 'no significant or fundamental changes' in the BJP-led Government's nuclear policy and that BJP-led India would not take any major strategic initiative (such as overt nuclearisation, strategic alliance with the United States, or support to Tibetan independence).

Although the aspirations for major power status are held by almost all Indian political parties (barring the Communists who fear provoking their Chinese masters), the BJP covets that status most ardently and is the most willing to assert it through military policy. Beijing would prefer a non-BJP weak government like the left-dominated United Front (UF) government before Pokhran II, and the successive Congress governments that preceded it, which had fine-tuned Sino-Indian bilateral relations by playing second fiddle to an assertive China. A policy paper prepared for the Chinese leadership has recommended 'targeting the BJP' as its policies have eroded Beijing's leverage against New Delhi. One analyst compared India with Nazi Germany and Iraq arguing that since the end of the Cold War, India had become too powerful and ambitious (for example, demanding a permanent seat on the UN Security Council) and warned that if India does not wish to suffer the fate of Japan in the 1940s or Iraq in the 1990s, it should give up its ambition for regional hegemony and take concrete steps to improve relations with China.

The main objective of China's Asia policy has always been to prevent the rise of an Asian rival or peer competitor to challenge its status as the Asia-Pacific's sole 'Middle Kingdom'. As an old Chinese saying goes, 'one mountain cannot accommodate two tigers'. That China does not want India to emerge as an equal is evident from its staunch opposition to India's membership of the P-5 (UN Security Council), N-5 (Nuclear Club), ASEM (Asia-Europe Summit), and APEC (Asia-Pacific Economic Cooperation). (India was made the ARF (ASEAN Regional Forum) member in December 1995 despite Beijing's opposition to it.) Speaking at the Munich Security Conference in February 1999, India's National Security Advisor, Brajesh Mishra, hinted at the BJP government's much broader political ambition by predicting that 'in the 21st century a new security order is likely to arise in the Asia-Pacific region in which India should be granted as much respect and deference by the United States and others as is China today.' Beijing's India-watchers believe that only a firm policy based on absolute strength and proactive containment of India will force the BJP-led government to act soberly towards China. Beijing knows that while China's emergence as a great power has been accepted by Western and Asian nations, India's claim to great power is yet to be accepted. So it is in the CCP's interests to keep the

BJP out of power. Beijing has been blamed by India's intelligence agencies, media and some politicians for the overthrow of the BJP-led government in April 1999. Strange as it may seem, the CCP has more in common with its bete noire, BJP, than its counterpart in India, the Communist Party of India-Marxist (CPM). In the BJP, the CCP has met its match, the latter's 'communist' pretensions notwithstanding. Contrary to the popular conception of the CCP and the BJP occupying opposite ends of the political spectrum, the BJP is the CCP's mirror image. Just as the CCP believes in the superiority of the Han race, Han civilisation and the Han culture while displaying patronising and condescending attitude towards minorities such as Tibetans, Mongols and Muslims and downplaying the repeated colonisation of the Han race first by Inner Asian tribes such as Mongols, Manchus and Hsingnus and then by the Europeans, the BJP believes in the superiority of the Hindu race, Hindu civilisation and Hindu culture while downplaying the repeated colonisation of India by Greek, Muslim and European invaders as a result of Hindu disunity and their contributions to Indian culture. What is more, the CCP's goal of a unified 'Greater China' is not much different from the RSS/BJP's dream of 'Akhand Bharat' (United India).

Just as the Chinese Communists lay claim to territories annexed by non-Chinese Mongol and Manchu empires (such as Tibet, Eastern Turkestan, Mongolia), the 'Akhand Bharat' concept includes territories (such as Burma and Sri Lanka) brought under control by the British. Much like the CCP, the BJP wants India to be an economic and military superpower in order to 'stand up' to great powers' bullying and coercion. Both have long nurtured the belief that as the two oldest civilisations and once great powers which were subjected to centuries of foreign domination, they must acquire the full spectrum of economic, technological and military (conventional, nuclear and information warfare) capabilities in order to be dominant regionally and influential globally.

Furthermore, the BJP's slogan of 'prosperous and powerful country' bears remarkable resemblance to the CCP's national goal: 'rich country, strong military' (fuguo qiangbing). Interestingly, both are courting the United States to help balance their relationships with each other until they are strong enough to do so on their own. Both want a new international status that is commensurate with their size, strength and potential. Historically and civilisationally, while China was the 'Middle Kingdom' of eastern Asia, India was the 'Middle Kingdom' of southern Asia.

The two parties are thus manifestation of the growing nationalism in India and China. Both also share remarkable similarity in economic outlooks and rhetorical excess. The BJP-led government is as aggressive in the pursuit of national interests as the CCP. Nor is it shy of flexing muscles and warning neighbours with 'serious consequences' if they don't behave-just as the Chinese Communists have always done! Although both the CCP and BJP have been labelled 'fascist', 'militarist' and 'ultra-natonalist' parties by their critics, the reality is that both are nationalist parties deeply conscious of their countries' history, culture and civilisational heritage to humankind and committed to restoring their countries' great power status. Both China after a century and India after a millenium of decline are keen to assume the great power roles they believe to be their historical and civilisational right. Both remain suspicious of each other's long-term agenda and intentions, and are attempting to fill any perceived power vacuum or block the other from doing so.

At the heart of Sino-Indian antagonism is the familiar Indian suspicion, which has now matured into a certainty, that China is seeking to deny India its proper stakes in the game of international politics. Both see themselves as newly rising great Asian powers whose time has finally come. This means that BJP's resurgent India will face CCP's rising China which will ensure a conflict of interests between the two giants unless their power competition is managed carefully. Their underlying power rivalry and their self-images as natural great powers and centres of civilisation and culture will continue to drive them to support different countries and causes. India versus

China, not India versus Pakistan, has always been the main game in Asia. However, post-colonial Asia has not experienced both a strong China and a strong India at the same time. The BJP-CCP clash is borne not out of conflicting, but complementary, visions for their respective countries.

INDIA AND CHINA TELL TROOPS TO STAND DOWN IN DISPUTED DOKLAM PLATEAU

India and China have agreed to an "expeditious disengagement" of troops in a disputed border area where their soldiers have been locked in a stand-off for more than two months, India's foreign ministry said on Monday. The decision comes ahead of a summit of the BRICS nations - a grouping that also includes Brazil, Russia and South Africa - in China next month, which Indian Prime Minister Narendra Modi is expected to attend.

Indian and Chinese troops have been confronting each other at the Doklam plateau near the borders of India, its ally Bhutan and China, in the most serious and prolonged standoff in decades along their disputed Himalayan border. The Indian ministry said the two sides had agreed to defuse the crisis following diplomatic talks. India-China tensions escalate as soldiers hurl stones at each other in "In recent weeks, India and China have maintained diplomatic communication in respect of the incident at Doklam," the ministry said in a statement. "On this basis, expeditious disengagement of border personnel at the face-off site at Doklam has been agreed to and is on-going," it said in a statement. It did not offer more details of the terms of disengagement from the area which had raised fears of a wider conflict between the Asian giants who fought a brief border war in 1962. China said Indian troops had withdrawn from the remote area in the eastern Himalayas. Chinese foreign ministry spokeswoman Hua Chunying said Chinese troops would continue to patrol the Doklam region. "China will continue to exercise sovereignty rights to protect territorial sovereignty in accordance with the rules of the historical boundary," she said. India and China have been unable to settle their 3,500-km (2,175-mile) frontier and large parts of territory are claimed by both sides.

"China hopes India respects the historical boundary and works with China to protect peace along the border on the basis of mutual respect of each other's sovereignty," Hua added. The trouble started in June when India sent troops to stop China building a road in the Doklam area, which is remote, uninhabited territory claimed by both China and Bhutan. India said it sent its troops because Chinese military activity there was a threat to the security of its own northeast region.

But China has said India had no role to play in the area and insisted it withdraw unilaterally or face the prospect of an escalation. Chinese state media had warned India of a fate worse than its crushing defeat in the war in 1962. Indian political commentator Shekhar Gupta said there was too much at stake for the two countries to fight over a small piece of territory. "Hopefully, Doklam is a new chapter in India-China relations. Too much at stake for both big powers to let legacy real-estate issues linger," he said in a Twitter post.

CHINA'S OBJECTIVES IN THE DOKLAM DISPUTE

At 14,000 feet above sea level and with a perpetually harsh climate, the Doklam Plateau is an enormously difficult place to defend. Meanwhile, those launching an attack face exponentially greatér challenges—and that's before the Himalayan winter sets in.

This helps explain why China and India last week ended a military standoff there that had been festering since June. Beyond the sheer misery of preparing to fight on such a forbidding battlefield, however, both nations had every reason to deescalate one of the most serious showdowns since their sole war in 1962. The *status quo ante* has been essentially restored, but the dispute raised important questions about the balance of power in Asia, China's grand strategy, and what Washington can learn from the episode.

China and India share a border over 2,500 miles long, with almost all of it based on colonial-era agreements and surveys, and much of it still disputed. China claims pieces of territory held by India, mostly in the states of Arunachal Pradesh and Jammu and Kashmir, with smaller pieces claimed in Uttarakhand and Himachal Pradesh. India claims land held by China, most notably a piece of land called Aksai Chin through which Beijing built a road in the 1950s connecting Xinjiang to Tibet. Reflecting its unsettled nature, the portions of the border separating disputed territories are referred to as the Line of Actual Control. There are periodic skirmishes along the LAC, but both nations have carefully choreographed them to avoid escalation; as a result, there have been no casualties stemming from land disputes in half a century.

On June 8, a platoon-sized unit of Chinese border guards moved into territory claimed by both China and Bhutan, a client-state of India. They destroyed stone bunkers used sporadically by the Royal Bhutan Army, and shortly afterward a Chinese road construction crew arrived with excavators, bulldozers, and a larger military escort. On June 16, Indian troops arrived and blocked the road-building effort. The next two months saw periodic scuffles at Doklam, as well as a mass rock-fight (captured on video and posted to YouTube) by the disputed banks of the Pangong Lake 800 miles away. On August 28, both nations agreed to what India termed an "expeditious disengagement" of forces, and both declared this non-resolution a victory.

INDIA V. CHINA: IT'S A MEXICAN STANDOFF

India is now the belle of the ball, as most of the world and Asian regional powers make pilgrimages to New Delhi to flatter and flirt with India's dynamic Prime Minister, Narendra Modi. Modi and India come with a certain amount of unpleasant baggage, which its suitors do their best to ignore. Modi himself is an unrepentant Hindutva cultural chauvinist whose attitudes toward Muslims (and convincing circumstantial evidence of his involvement in an anti-Muslim pogrom in Gujarat—so convincing, in fact, he was previously banned from the United States) trend toward the fascistic.

In regional affairs, India has not been a particularly responsible or constructive actor, having mixed it up with Pakistan (abetted the split-off of East Pakistan a.ka. Bangladesh), Nepal (opened the door to the Nepalese Communists with its inept deposition of the King), and Sikkim (Sikkim, in case you noticed, doesn't exist anymore; it was annexed by India in 1975) and presided over a bloody insurgency and brutal counterinsurgency in Kashmir that has claimed the lives of at least 60,000 people. India birthed the horrific Tamil Tiger insurgency in Sri Lanka and its intelligence services played what may have been a decisive role in organizing and executing the successful electoral challenge on January 8, 2015, to the rule of the pro-Chinese (now-ex) president of Sri Lanka, Mahinda Rajapaksa.

And there's the People's Republic of China, and the contested issue of the borderlands of Arunachal Pradesh in the northeast and Aksai Chin in the northwest. Japan's Foreign Minister, Fumio Kishida, got himself tangled up in the Arunachal Pradesh issue during his recent visit to India.

China today lodged a protest with Tokyo after Japan's foreign minister was quoted as saying that Arunachal Pradesh was "India's territory." Japan's Sankei Shimbun, a conservative daily, quoted Fumio Kishida as having made the remarks in New Delhi on Saturday. Japan played down the issue today, saying it could not confirm Kishida's reported remarks. It added that it hoped India and China could resolve their border dispute peacefully. Kishida's reported remarks drew an angry response from China, which called on Tokyo to "understand the sensitivity of the Sino-India boundary issue."

A Japanese foreign ministry spokesperson said "the statement was made considering the reality that Arunachal Pradesh state is basically in reality controlled by India and that China and India are continuing negotiations over the border dispute." China disputes the entire territory of Arunachal, calling it south Tibet, especially Tawang, a key site for Tibetan Buddhism. The historic town briefly fell into Chinese hands during their 1962 war before Beijing retreated.

The Japanese Foreign Ministry backtracked expeditiously, indicating that Kishida's remarks were perhaps a slip of the tongue and not meant to inject Japan into the Arunachal Pradesh issue. Ever since Prime Minister Abe returned to office with an India-centric Asian policy, yearnings have been expressed that Japan might openly side with India on the Arunachal Pradesh issue. The PRC, was extremely leery of previous PM Manmohan Singh and his overt diplomatic and emotional tilt toward Japan and, with good reason, has expected the current officeholder, Nadendra Modi, to play off China, Russia, and the United States in a more pragmatic manner.

This, indeed, was the takeaway from President Obama's recently concluded trip to India. President Obama's decision to accept Prime Minister Modhi's invitation to attend the Republic Day extravaganza further buttressed Modi's prestige and popularity within India and elicited a wave of "Mobama" triumphalism in the press, much to China's discomfiture. However, in the end, Modi played true to form by publicly and bluntly rejecting President Obama's call to limit India's greenhouse gas emissions.

For the PRC, an important area of anxiety is Arunachal Pradesh and the threat that India might "internationalize" the bilateral border dispute by canvassing its actual and would-be allies for support on the issue; perhaps even to the extent of going tit-for-tat with Japan i.e. India backing Japan on the issue of Senkaku sovereignty in return for Japanese aid and comfort on AP. However, it looks like Japan—like the Asian Development Bank, which ran into a PRC buzzsaw when it tried to put an Arunachal Pradesh hydropower project on its agenda in 2009—is not quite ready to mix it up on AP.

Let's unpack the Arunachal Pradesh issue. I've written a lot about Arunachal Pradesh. It's a complicated situation and I scattered my narrative over a handful of posts: "China 'pivot' trips over McMahon Line," "Charm Offensive: China's Flank of Discontent," and "India Places Its Asian Bet on Japan: Roiling the Waters of the Asia-Pacific."

To summarize. Arunachal Pradesh is a region controlled by India in its northeast quadrant, between Bhutan and Burma, home to a variety of ethnic groups. One of those groups is Tibetan, centred on the town and district of Tawang in the western end of AP at the border with Bhutan.

The Arunachal Pradesh dispute is bookended with Aksai Chin, a blasted desert between India and the PRC in the northwest, and is controlled by the PRC. The Indian claim to Aksai Chin is not terribly robust, since it is based on an internal British Indian survey—the Johnson Line—which was never discussed or agreed with China. The PRC built a strategic road across Aksai Chin in the 1950s, and it took several years for the Indian government to even find out it was there.

There is a third slice of disputed territory, the "Trans-Karakorum Tract" bordering Kashmir, geographically distinct from Aksai Chin, which India claims Pakistan illegally ceded to the PRC in a land swap. For some reason, the PRC and India aren't arguing about this piece. Both Arunachal Pradesh (AP) and Aksai Chin territories have been openly disputed since before the 1962 Sino-Indian war. The PRC has at times offered a grand bargain in which the two sides acknowledge each other's regions of effective control, by which India got AP and the PRC gets AC. The official Indian response has been nothing doing and all territory it lost in the 1962 war must be recovered i.e. Aksai Chin is not negotiable. It has decoupled the two issues, and has focused its diplomacy on the insistence that its sovereignty over AP be confirmed. India's claim to AP is complicated in an interesting way.

In 1914, Great Britain was interested in creating an autonomous Tibetan buffer—"Outer Tibet"—between British India and Russia/China. To this end, Sir Henry McMahon, the Foreign Minister of British India, invited Tibetan and Republic of China delegates to the Indian town of Simla. Tibet, eager to be acknowledged as an autonomous power with its own rights to negotiate directly with foreign powers (and not just through China), generously conceded a delineation of Lhasa's sphere of control—the McMahon Line–that alienated Tawang, a market town that interested the Raj, to British India.

However, the Simla Agreement was negotiated between the Tibetan and British representatives in a provisional sort of way after the Chinese representatives had packed up and left. Since Britain's Foreign Office was protective of its China diplomacy and not interested in encouraging Tibetan pretensions to negotiate as an independent sovereign power, the absence of the Chinese representatives—and a Chinese endorsement of the border arrangement accepted by the Tibetan authorities– was a deal breaker.

The Simla Agreement was apparently treated as an aspirational document and was recorded in the most authoritative compendium of British Indian treaties, Sir Charles Umpherston Aitchison's Collection of Treaties, Engagements, and Sanads, with the notation that neither Great Britain nor China had ratified the treaty. Since Tibet wasn't recognized as a sovereign power, whatever it hoped to achieve with the Simla Accord—and what it had tried to give away, namely Tawang– was, in the eyes of the British, moot.

Things puttered along until 1935, when the detention of a British spy in Tawang by Tibetan authorities awakened the cupidity of a diplomat in the Foreign Office of British India, Olaf Caroe. Caroe checked the files, found that Great Britain had no ratified claims on Tawang, and decided to amend and improve the record. He arranged for the relevant original volume of the 1929 Aitchison compendium to be withdrawn from the various libraries in which it was filed, discarded, and replaced with a new version—but one that still claimed to be compiled in 1929, thereby removing the need for awkward explanations or documentation concerning why the switch had happened. The spurious version claimed that Tibet and Britain had accepted the treaty.

The deception was only discovered in 1964, when a researcher was able to compare one of the last three surviving copies of the original compendium, at Harvard University, with the spurious replacement. Unfortunately, that was too late for Nehru, who staked his security strategy and his diplomatic exchanges with China to a significant extent on the fallacy that he had inherited from British India a clear and unequivocal claim to its borders.

In 1962 Nehru decided to move up military units to assert India's claim to territory in Ladakh/Aksai Chin and up to the McMahon Line in Arunachal Pradesh under a gambit optimistically named The Forward Policy. The PRC begged to differ—and Chairman Mao was itching to stick it to India's patron, Nikita Khrushchev–and attacked. India's entire strategy had been predicated on the assumption that the PRC would not respond (shades, I think, of Western confidence that Vladimir Putin would stay his hand in eastern Ukraine out of fear of sanctions and the wrath of his impoverished and disgruntled oligarchs) and the Indian Army, outnumbered, undersupplied, and disorganized, was completely unprepared to fight for the high ground in the north. India suffered a humiliating defeat at the hands of the PLA. After its victory, the PRC decided to take the high ground, diplomatically as well as geographically. It withdrew its forces to behind the McMahon Line and offered a swap of AP for AC. No dice, as we have seen. India clearly does not see any need to credit AP—territory that the PRC abandoned—as any kind of bargaining chip concerning Aksai Chin. This is, perhaps, a cautionary tale to the PRC as to the geostrategic minuses as well as pluses of trying to behave like Mr. Nice Guy.

This history is officially persona non grata in India. The report the Indian government commissioned on the 1962 war—the Henderson Brooks Report–was so devastating to India's position and its legal, military, and diplomatic pretensions it was promptly banned and publication is forbidden to this day. In an ironic recapitulation of the case of the Atchison compendium, it was assumed that there were only two typewritten copies and they were securely buttoned up in safes in New Delhi. However, the Times of London correspondent, Neville Maxwell, got his hands on a copy and used it to write an expose on the tragedy of errors in 1962, India's China War, thereby earning himself the fierce hatred of generations of Indian nationalists.

Maxwell tried several times to put the report into the public domain. As quoted in Outlook India, Maxwell provided an interesting account of how the freedom of expression sausage gets made when the information involved is not necessarily a matter of national security (the report is classified Top Secret, but its content—the minutiae of military decisions and movements sixty years ago have no current strategic or tactical significance) but is a matter of supreme political embarrassment (to Nehru, the Congress Party, the Gandhi political dynasty, and to the army).

My first attempt to put the Report itself on the public record was indirect and low-key: after I retired from the University I donated my copy to Oxford's Bodleian Library, where, I thought, it could be studied in a setting of scholarly calm. The Library initially welcomed it as a valuable contribution in that "grey area" between actions and printed books, in which I had given them material previously. But after some months the librarian to whom I had entrusted it warned me that, under a new regulation, before the Report was put on to the shelves and opened to the public it would have to be cleared by the British government with the government which might be adversely interested! Shocked by that admission of a secret process of censorship to which the Bodleian had supinely acceded I protested to the head Librarian, then an American, but received no response. Fortunately I was able to retrieve my donation before the Indian High Commission in London was alerted in the Bodleian's procedures and was perhaps given the Report.

In 2002, noting that all attempts in India to make the government release the Report had failed, I decided on a more direct approach and made the text available to the editors of three of India's leading publications, asking that they observe the usual journalistic practice of keeping their source to themselves...To my surprise the editors concerned decided, unanimously, not to publish...Later I gave the text to a fourth editor and offered it to a fifth, with the same nil result.

Narendra Modi, a determined foe of the Congress Party and the Gandhis (I had to chuckle when I read these fawning articles about President Obama bonding with Prime Minister Modi over their shared Gandhi love, despite the awkward fact that Modi's BJP nationalist party had been and apparently still is the spiritual home of Gandhi's assassin), came to power promising to release the report,but didn't. And when Maxwell posted part of the report on his website, the site was symbolically blocked.

The Indian army, in particular, is wedded to a creation myth of PRC perfidy that is infinitely more utile than acknowledging that the PLA attack, rather than unprovoked, was a response to a strategically and diplomatically bankrupt Indian border gambit compounded by non-stop miscues by India's civilian leadership and a disastrous defeat for its military forces.

In 2005, the PRC and India started negotiations over the borders issue. Here's a nice explainer from the Daily Mail! in 2013 which signals that Aksai Chin might be on the table, but Tawang is off the table, and unfortunately omits the significant complication of the Caroe forgery.

India's move into Arunachal Pradesh in the 1950s is less than a slam dunk according to international law, complicated in particular by the issue of Tawang. Not only is there the problem of Olaf Caroe's bibliographic hijinks, there is the awkward fact that India forcefully displaced Tibetan theocratic rule in Tawang—nominally rule from Lhasa, actually local rule by the immensely powerful monastery.

Lhasa had apparently experienced cartographic remorse over Simla and implored India to recognize Tawang as Tibetan territory in 1947. Instead, India seized the district in 1951 in-a quasi-official/quasi-military "liberating the Tibetan serfs" operation rather similar to what the PRC conducted in its part of Tibet.

In recent years, the Dalai Lama has been forced into the unpleasant position of affirming Indian sovereignty over Tawang, whose great monastery (the second largest in Tibetan Buddhism) first gave him shelter when he fled PRC control in 1959, and which had hosted the reincarnation of the 6th Dalai Lama way back when.

The Dalai Lama apparently verbally acknowledged, if not in writing, that AP and Tawang belonged to India on several occasions while he still served at the apex of power in the Tibetan government in exile (a position he relinquished in 2011). However, I assume twisting the Dalai Lama's arm to concede Indian sovereignty over Tawang falls a little bit short, since the Tibetan government-in-exile lacks international recognition (and with it the right to cede territory to India).

The PRC is happy to harp on Tawang's role in the AP situation, since it serves as a continual reminder that India is occupying territory in AP that, however you slice it, is a core component of the Tibetan homeland, thereby keeping alive a non-Indian or, if you want, a PRC-cum-Tibet claim to at least part of the region and attempting to balk India's attempt to claim full sovereignty over Arunachal Pradesh under international law.

To understand how this relates to the Senkakus requires reflection on another piece of suppressed history—that the United States returned the Senkakus to Japanese administrative control not sovereignty in 1973 as part of the Okinawa package with the stated expectation that the sovereignty of the rocks would be negotiated between China and Japan.

My personal opinion is that the PRC is in no hurry to unfreeze the conflict over Arunachal Pradesh, and its insistence on sovereignty over Tawang—a district, I suspect, that has extremely limited interest in reunification with the Chinese motherland—is something of a pretext. With the Simla Agreement tainted and no subsequent cession of Tawang by Tibet or China, the Indian position in Tawang is embarrassingly similar to that of the PRC in the matter of the Spratlys i.e. having expelled the previous rulers by conquest and achieved control of the territory without attaining international recognition of its sovereignty.

And it's somewhat similar to the Senkakus, where the United States effectively surrendered its sovereignty over the islands when it returned Okinawa and the Ryukyus to Japan, but didn't cede its claim to anybody else.

Maybe Arunachal Pradesh is another one of those Mexican-standoff situations like Kashmir vs. Tibet (a.k.a. the Indian temptation to make mischief in the ethnic-Tibetan areas of the PRC is inhibited by concern that the PRC, via Pakistan, might light the fuse in Kashmir).

The PRC keeps the Tawang/AP issue alive to forestall thoughts by India of giving aid and comfort to Japan on the Senkakus or, for that matter, Vietnam on the Spratlys.

Both the PRC and India are bulking up their infrastructure and military on their respective sides of the de facto McMahon-Line-based border, making it a virtual certainty that India will never alienate any part of AP, including Tawang. That's good news for reduced actual tensions (as opposed to defence ministry posturing) at the shared border, but India's heightened sense of security concerning Arunachal Pradesh may encourage it to be less tentative vis a vis the PRC in its Japanese and Vietnamese diplomacy.

Bibliography

Allen Carlson, *Unifying China, Integrating with the World: Securing Chinese Sovereignty in the Reform Era,* Stanford: Stanford University Press, 2005.

Bhat, T.P. : *India and China : Trade Complementarities and Competitiveness,* Bookwell, Delhi, 2008.

Chandra, R.: *Judicial System in Mechanical Warfare,* Lucknow, Print House (India), 1992.

Coakley, J.: *The Territorial Management of Ethnic Conflict,* London: Frank Cass, 2003.

Deepak, B R : *India and China : 1904-2004 : A Century of Peace and Conflict,* Manak, Delhi, 2005.

Erik H.: *Gandhi's Truth: On the Origins of Militant Nonviolence,* W. W. Norton, New York, 1969.

Evelyn Goh, *Meeting the China Challenge: The U.S. in Southeast Asian Regional Security Strategies,* DC: East-West Center, 2005.

Faure, Bernard : *The Will to Orthodoxy: A Critical Genealogy of Northern Chan Buddhism,* Stanford, CA: Stanford University Press, 1997.

Gupta, Asha: *Military Rule and Democratization : Changing Perspectives,* Deep & Deep, Delhi, 2003.

Gupta, S.: *Disrupted Borders: An Intervention in Definitions of Boundaries,* London: River Oram Press, 1993.

Heimanson, Rudolph: *Dictionary of Military,* N.Y.: Oceana Publications, 1967.

Ian Storey: *ASEAN and the South China Sea: Movement in Lieu of Progress,* Washington, D.C., Jamestown Foundation,2012.

Jha, Prem Shankar : *India and China : The Battle Between Soft and Hard Power,* Penguin Books India, Delhi, 2010.

John McRae: *The Northern School and the Formation of Early Ch'an Buddhism,* Honolulu, HI: University of Hawaii Press, 1984.

Jones, W.H.: *Politics of Military,* London, Hutchinson, 1971.

Joon Ahn: *The Rise of China and the Future of East Asian Integration*, Asia-Pacific Review, London, Carfax Publishing Company, 2004.

Kudaisya, Gyanesh: *The Aftermath of Partition in South Asia*. London: Routledge, 2000.

Kumar, Satish. *Rana Polity in Nepal: Origin and Growth*. New York: Asia, 1967.

Kunju, N. : *Indo-Pak : Nuclear Cold War*, Reliance, Delhi, 2002.

Lamrimpa, Gen : *Realizing Emptiness: Madhyamaka Insight Meditation*, Ithaca, NY: Snow Lion, 2002.

Lohia, Ram Manohar: *Guilty Men of India's Partition*. Allahabad: Navahind, 1960.

Major Donovan: *Air Defence Power*. Sampson Low. London, 1940.

Marie Lecomte : *Hindu Kingship, Ethnic Revival, and Maoist Rebellion in Nepal*, Oxford University Press, Delhi, 2009.

Narendra K Dash : *Buddhism in Indian Literature*, Aryan Books International, 2007.

Nevile, P.: *Lahore: A Sentimental Journey*. New Delhi: Penguin, 1993.

Nishioka Keiji : *Flowers of Bhutan*, Asahi Shimbum, Tokyo, 1984.

Olschak Blanche : *Ancient Bhutan: a Study on Early Buddhism in the Himalayas*, Swiss Foundation for Alpine Research 1979.

Prabir De: *India and China in an Era of Globalisation : Essays on Economic Cooperation*, Bookwell, Delhi, 2005.

Raj Kumar: *Weapons and Military Technology*, Sumit Enterprises, Delhi, 2009.

Robert M Cassidy: *Counterinsurgency and the Global War on Terror : Military Culture and Irregular War*, Pentagon Press, Delhi, 2008.

Rosen, P.: *Societies and Military Power: India and its Armies*, Ithaca, Cornell University Press, 1996.

Samuel P. Huntington: *The Soldier and the State : The Theory and Politics of Civil-Military Relations*, Natraj Pub, Delhi, 2005.

Thampi, Madhavi : *India and China in the Colonial World*, Social Science Press, Delhi, 2010.

Wakamiya Yoshibumi, *The Postwar Conservative View of Asia*, Tokyo: LTCB International Library Foundation, 1999.

Index

N

P

R

S

W

❑❑❑